God bless,

Hanna Johnson

SAYS WHO?

THINGS THAT CAN KNOCK YOU OFF YOUR GOAL
⤙ AND ⤚
WHAT YOU CAN DO ABOUT THEM

JOHNNIE JOHNSON

For permission requests, contact the publisher at:

Growing Tree Learning Center, Inc.
DBA World Class Coaches
3540 W. Sahara Ave. #780
Las Vegas, NV 89102
800-314-7713
Fax 702-920-7655
www.worldclasscoaches.com

Second edition. Printed in the United States of America

Self-Help/Inspirational   US $19.95
ISBN.0-9772629-0-1

Contents

Says Who?

Acknowledgements

I give thanks to the Good Lord for His grace and for blessing me with a wonderful wife in Julie Johnson, and for blessing the Johnson household with three wonderful kids in Kirk Anthony, Collin Wayne, and Camille Marie.

I give thanks to my dear, departed mother, Jessie Mae Johnson, who taught me about the power of faith and the strength of prayer.

Mother, you also taught me about the power of believing—the simple faith that if you want to accomplish something, you must start first with a crystal-clear vision, put forth your maximum effort, and not be afraid of failure. Mom, one of your favorite sayings will be with me for the rest of my life, "Why worry when you can pray."

I give thanks to the World Class Coaches' team of professionals, its affiliates and partners. We are grateful for the opportunity to reach out and touch so many different people around the world and the unique opportunity of assisting them in realizing more of their God-given potential.

I give thanks to my football coaches—Ben Bloomer, Darrel Royal, Fred Akers, Ray Malavasi, John Robinson, and Chuck Knox—for helping me to grow personally, on and off the field. I give thanks to my good friend, mentor, and life coach, Lou Tice, for teaching me that the playing field in the game of life is the world. Thank you for the daily influence you continue to have on my life.

I give thanks to Ken Shelton, Editor-in-Chief at Executive Excellence Publishing, for his professionalism, leadership, editing and the many wonderful suggestions he provides in a total selfless way. Ken, I thank you for being such a great man of high morals and character.

I give thanks to Benjamin Devey, Production Manager of Executive Excellence Publishing, for the expertise he brought to the concept and design of this book. Thank you for all the wonderful support you provide me and for your high degree of integrity.

Introduction

The purpose of this book is to assist you in creating the necessary focus and direction to overcome obstacles or barriers in your life that can knock you off your goal.

Says Who? will provide you with success strategies and critical thinking skills to assist you in staying focused on your goals and confident in your ability to achieve them.

What sets highly effective people and high-performance individuals apart from those who perform at a lower level? Why is it that some people seem to consistently utilize more of their God-given potential and realize more of their goals, while others fail to do so?

Many of the answers can be found in how they deal with those things that tend to knock them off their goals.

It's fairly easy to keep your sight on your goals when things are going well. However, one of the vital keys to ultimately accomplishing your vision will be how well you remain focused on your goals when you feel your life is in chaos, or when someone casts doubt on your ability to achieve them. When things are not going as planned, you are most susceptible to handing over the power and the control of your goals to a circumstance in your life, or to someone else who may be operating on limited information or limited thinking.

The success strategies and critical thinking skills used by world-class athletes, high-performance individuals, and other highly effective people enable them to remain focused on their goals and confi-

dent in their abilities to achieve them, despite their circumstances, things not going as planned, or the comments they hear from others.

Says Who? will provide you with the concepts and success strategies you need to become a highly effective, high-performance individual. These concepts and strategies will enable you to remain focused on your goals and realize your vision, despite your circumstances, competition, opposition, failures, doubts, or fears.

Section 1
Start Where You Are

When I was growing up in a poor family in La Grange, Texas, my Mom, a single mother with 11 children, would talk to us about not allowing anyone to talk us out of our goals just because of our circumstances. A passionate believer in God and strong in her faith, she taught us about the power of having a vision, setting goals, and having faith.

My mother was wise in her thinking. She often said that with a strong vision, clearly defined goals and God's will and grace, you can achieve anything you desire—if you stay focused on your goals, do not rationalize or make excuses when things are not going as planned, and be careful who you listen to when you're facing adversity. She often talked about the importance of overcoming objections and keeping your sights on your vision when you find yourself in the midst of a storm.

Her words continue to ring through my ears today. I wasn't aware of it at the time, but when I look back on it, my Mom was teaching success strategies and critical thinking skills used by world-class athletes, high-performance individuals, and other highly effective people. I believe that God does not place limitations on any of us; we either place them on ourselves or we allow others to place them on us.

I start with this story as a tribute to my mother.

Chapter 1
God Has a Plan for You

As a young teenager growing up in La Grange, Texas, a number of things transpired that greatly impacted my life and could easily have knocked me off my goals.

For starters, when I was 13 years old, my Dad walked out on my Mom, leaving her to raise five of their 11 children alone. They were later divorced.

Even today, deep down inside, I have this knot in my stomach from the pain of experiencing the divorce of my parents. All I can say is, thank God for my wonderful mother. She dedicated her life to raising her kids to the best of her ability, with what few resources she had to work with.

One resource was government-assistance programs. I grew up on the welfare system. I can recall going with my Mom to pick-up cheese, powdered milk, and other free food through the welfare program.

But the primary resource we had to rely on was my mother's love and leadership. Mom led by example! The house we lived in was a small, wooden-frame home with no indoor plumbing. The house had a tin roof and was heated by a wood-burning stove. As kids, we often woke up during cold Texas winter mornings to the heat of the stove from the fire my Mom had made and the smell of bacon cooking for breakfast.

Each family member had specific chores to do, and Mom made it very clear that the rest of the family was relying on each of us to fulfill our family responsibilities. No exceptions, and no excuses.

As I saw how hard my Mom worked to care for the family, I felt a need to provide more assistance to boost her efforts. So I decided to take a summer job doing farm work. On pay day, I would take each dollar earned and give it to her to help provide for the family. My contribution was small, but Mom made me feel so big.

Scriptures for Stress

I continued doing this for a while when all of a sudden I felt my life was crashing in on me. I felt the pressures of all that was going on with the family. What was expected of me at such a young age was at times overwhelming.

These stressful feelings led to a series of cherished conversations between me and my Mom. One of those chats covered the importance of having a mission and vision in life, despite your circumstances.

I said, "Mom, there must be a better way of life. I don't know how much more of this I can take!"

In a very cool and calm manner, she said, "Son, do you believe that there's a God?"

I replied, "Yes!"

She left the room for a moment and returned with her Bible! The Bible was Mom's playbook. She asked me to read out loud the following scriptures:

Proverbs 29:18: "Where there is no vision, the people perish: but he that keepeth the law, happy is he."

Hebrews 11:1: "Now faith is the substance of things hoped for, the evidence of things not seen."

Hebrews 11:6: "But without faith, it is impossible to please Him, for he who comes to God must believe that He is, and He is a rewarder of those who diligently seek Him.

Joshua 1:9: "Have I not commanded you? Be strong and of good courage: do not be afraid, nor be dismayed, for the Lord your God is with you wherever you go."

James 1:2-3: "My brethren, count it all joy when you fall into various trials; knowing that the testing of your faith produces patience."

Mark 11:25: "And whenever you stand praying, if you hold anything against anyone, forgive him, so that your Father in heaven may forgive you your sins."

Hebrews 12:1 "Since we are surrounded by so great a cloud of witnesses, let us lay aside every weight, and the sin which so easily ensnares us, and let us run with endurance the race that is set before us."

James 1:5-6 "If any of you lacks wisdom, let him ask God, who gives to all liberally and without reproach and it will be given to him. But let him ask in faith, with no doubting, for he who doubts is like a wave of the sea driven and tossed by the wind."

2 Corinthians 5:7: "For we walk by faith, not by sight."

Beyond the Here and Now

As I read the scriptures, I asked her what they meant. She replied, "Son, God has a plan for you. He placed you here for a reason. It's important for you to find out why He placed you here.

"When you look around and see what's going on in your life today, you can easily become discouraged. It's easy to get all wrapped up in the here and now—the chaos going on in your life.

"However, those things should not drive your life. I encourage you to figure out your mission and vision in life and to be strong and of good courage in pursuing them, despite your circumstances or comments you hear from other people."

Chapter 2
What Is My Vision and Mission?

Now, this motherly advice sounded all fine and dandy, but I was having a real hard time seeing through all the difficulties we found ourselves in. From my point of view, we were just trying to survive from day to day. So I asked my Mom about her mission and vision in life.

She replied in a calm and confident manner, "God put me here for you kids," she said. "I envision raising my kids to be the best that they can be, and someday living in a brick home with a clothes line hanging between two large oak trees in the back yard. And on the clothes line, I envision clothes blowing in the wind during all seasons of the year."

When I heard her comments, I recall thinking to myself, "When was the last time the United States government purchased a person a brick home?" because based on the situation we were in, I felt that would be the only way we would ever have such a home.

I marveled that she could envision such a bright future with such clarity, having just been recently divorced and receiving government assistance to help feed her kids.

Nevertheless, I took her advice and tried first to remain strong and of good courage, because that is what I needed just to get through the next day.

As I continued taking Mom's advice, I noticed that my attitude started to change. I began to have a more positive outlook on life, even though I was not certain what was really driving the change.

Says Who?

A Sincere Interest in Sports

As my outlook on life began to change, I started to develop a sincere interest in sports. During this process, I discovered I was blessed with exceptional athletic ability. Although I was only 13 years old, at this time I made two of the best decisions of my life and one of the poorest decisions of my life. The two best decisions were when I set a goal to play pro football and when I chose sports over drugs, alcohol, and gangs. It was at this time that I had my first vision—to play in the National Football League.

Oddly enough, the vision I received was just as clear to me as Mom's vision of raising her kids to be the best that they could be and someday living in a brick home. I could clearly see myself playing in the National Football League. I could see myself as a professional football player with such clarity that at times I felt I was actually taking part in a game. I decided to put my vision in writing and read it almost daily. This step brought even more focus to my vision. It was very real to me.

Equipped with such a clear vision, I recall the enthusiasm and excitement I experienced anytime I thought about my vision, or talked about it to others.

Opposition in All Things

It was the talking about my vision that led me to making one of the poorest decisions of my life. That was when I told the people in La Grange about my goal of playing in the National Football League.

You see, when I set the goal, I was not aware that no one from La Grange had ever played major college football before, let alone pro football; and it did not take long for the people in La Grange to remind me of that fact. Many people stated that in their opinion, they just didn't see how it could be done. I heard, over and over, "If no one else has done it, what makes you think you can do it, especially when you look at your circumstances?"

Basically I heard all the reasons why I would not or could not accomplish my goals. In fact, I even had some of my relatives tell me that it was "for my own good" that I should not set my goals so high, because they did not want me to be disappointed when I failed to achieve them.

Upon entering high school, my circumstances at home did not change that much, nor did the opinions and comments I heard from many others regarding my goals; however, what did change were the opportunities that started to unfold before my eyes. They started early in sports, as my high school coaches placed me on the varsity as a freshman in three of the four high school sports I participated in during the year.

When I look back on it, this was significant in my life. It was the first time I could recall that someone other than my Mom and immediate family members demonstrated faith and confidence in me, in spite of my circumstances. The opportunities presented to me by my coaches enabled me to become more aware of some of my God-given talents.

And yet, their confidence in me also brought about a certain degree of fear, because I was not accustomed to anyone demonstrating such faith and confidence in me and my abilities. At times the fear seemed to be overwhelming.

This fear prompted me to once again seek the counsel of my mother.

Says Who?

I recall informing her that I felt I had really connected with the scriptures she had previously shared with me; however, because of

the great trust and confidence my coaches had placed in me, I was really scared. "What if I don't measure up? What if I let people down?" I asked her.

She replied by asking me, "*Who says* you are going to let anyone down?"

This question made me really think about why I was thinking the way I was thinking. Like most mothers, she seemingly knew exactly what to say at precisely the right moment. When I could not provide her with a logical answer, she then asked me a question that really made me think about what was causing me to feel the way I was feeling. She asked, "What has changed in your life that is causing you to feel the way you are feeling?"

When I thought about it, I could think of several things that had changed, and I shared those things with her. One of my main fears was letting my coaches down because of the confidence and trust they were placing in me. I felt a real need to please them by doing well. To complicate matters, I was being asked to perform at the varsity level, an expectation normally reserved for juniors and seniors, even though I was just a freshman. When I stood back and looked at it, I really felt out of my comfort zone.

Because of the need to please my coaches and to play outside of my comfort zone, and because of all the comments I was hearing from others who were casting doubts on my ability to achieve my goals, I felt tremendous pressure on my shoulders. In fact, I felt that the pressures were beginning to drive my life. They also started to affect my thought process, as those little voices in my head would at times cause me to approach something I loved so dearly in sports with a fear of making a mistake.

This approach was not in alignment with the way I understood we were to live our lives based on the scriptures my Mom had shared with me. That lead me to give more thought to the question: "What had changed in my life that was causing me to feel the way I was feeling?" I began to question why I was thinking the way I was thinking. What was really driving the way I was feeling?

Knowing what changes or circumstances in your life may be causing you to feel the way you do will enable you to remain focused on your goals.

What Has Changed?

In my case, I recall giving the "what has changed?" question some thought and decided to take my Mom's advice by identifying what had changed that was causing me to feel the way I was feeling. I came up with four things:

• Instead of playing with athletes my age as a freshman, the coaching staff had determined that God had granted me with certain gifts and talents worthy of playing sports with juniors and seniors in high school.

• Although I was just a freshman, my coaches demonstrated their faith and confidence in my ability to use those gifts and talents under any circumstance, even playing at the varsity level.

• Having never played at the varsity level before, I was horrified by a fear of the unknown and doubts about how I would fit in and perform at that level.

• For the first time, someone besides my Mom and family members had displayed a high level of trust and confidence in me.

When I took a look at what I had came up with, I was amazed! I was sure that there was more to it! The feelings of fear and doubt were so great that at times they seemed to paralyze me and prevent me from utilizing more of my natural God-given potential. They robbed me of pursuing something I loved dearly with passion.

Says Who?

However, after assessing the situation objectively, I determined that the only changes that had occurred in my life were those four conditions.

Chapter 3
Be the Best You Can Be

I decided to share what had changed in my life with my Mom.

True to form, she responded by asking me, "Where did you get those legs to run as fast as you can, or jump as high as you can jump?"

"From God," I replied.

She said, "We're all blessed in different ways. Son, you've started to recognize some of your gifts."

She paused, and I could feel the weight of her message. Then she delivered the "one liner" that changed my life: "Regardless of your situation, all I ask of you is to just be yourself, but *be the best you can be*, despite your circumstances."

Being the best Johnnie Johnson I could be was something I felt I could do. In fact, I was looking forward to it, because I wanted no part of whatever was causing all the stress and pressure in my life. It had caused me to become something I did not want to be.

Although Mom knew very little about sports, her comments were very much in alignment with the comments I had heard from my coaches. When Ben Bloomer, my high school football coach, first informed me that he had decided that I had the ability to play on the varsity team as a freshman, he asked if it was something I would like to pursue. He then said that all he wanted from me was for me to be my best self.

Do Only One Thing

In an effort to relieve some of the pressures I felt in my life and based on my belief that the scriptures my Mom shared with me would positively impact my life, I asked if she knew of any scriptures that could help me in the current situation I found myself in.

She then shared the following scriptures with me:

Matthew 5: 14-16: "You are the light of the world. A city that is set on a hill cannot be hidden. Nor do they light a lamp and put it under a basket, but on a lamp stand, and it gives light to all who are in the house. Let your light so shine before men, that they may see your good works and glorify your Father in heaven."

She then said, "I ask that you do only one thing: Do everything within your power to please God by letting your light shine."

Her words really hit home with me. Based on my belief in the God-given talents I was discovering, in my mothers advice, and in the confidence my coaches showed in me, I decided that there was a way I could honor God.

I said to myself: "I can best glorify God for granting me these gifts and talents by approaching each and every play in sports, whether it be practice or a game, with every ounce of energy and drive I had in my body—and let Him take care of the rest."

Whatever happened would be up to Him, but I was going to do my part by playing the game at the highest level possible at all times, regardless of the circumstances. I decided that I may not be able to control the circumstances; however, I could control my approach to them. I was not going to allow circumstances or the comments I heard from others to knock me off my goal.

Possibilities and Opportunities

With this positive approach to life, attending college started to become more of a possibility. While still a sophomore in high school, I received my first piece of recruiting literature—a questionnaire from the University of Notre Dame!

This was just the first of many such recruiting inquiries in four different sports. By my senior year in high school, I had received communication from over 100 different colleges and universities from around the country. Now I knew that I would have the opportunity to attend college on an athletic scholarship. Upon completing high school, I was awarded a full athletic scholarship in football by the University of Texas.

At the University of Texas, I was twice selected as an All-American defensive back, and I was projected to be a #1 draft pick in the annual National Football League player draft. My vision of playing in the NFL was about to be realized.

That projection became a reality when I became a #1 draft pick of the Los Angeles Rams. Although I had looked forward to that moment for at least eight years, when it finally occurred, I was stunned. My goal was to play in the National Football League, but how fortunate I felt to be a #1 draft pick.

Chapter 4
Vision Becomes Reality

At the very moment I was selected in the first round of the draft by the Rams, I thought about the conversation I had with my Mom as a young teenager. I just could not thank her enough for providing me with the guidance and coaching to enable me to stay focused on my goals, when so many things existed to knock me off them.

When I arrived in Los Angeles and signed my rookie contract with the Rams, opportunities continued to flow my way. As the team's first million-dollar player, I was overwhelmed with the thought and joy of finally being able to achieve another of the goals I set as a 13 year-old— that goal was to purchase my Mom a home. I had made a decision that the first money I earned from playing pro football was going to go toward purchasing her that brick home she envisioned.

That day soon arrived. When I returned to La Grange shortly after signing my NFL contract, I was able to purchase my Mom the brick home she dreamed about.

Words cannot really express the joy and peace I experienced when I presented her with the keys to her new home and thanked her for having as her life's purpose to raise her kids to be the best that they could be, despite what many considered to be over-whelming odds. I looked her right in the eyes and told her: "Mom, you have done enough in life. Now it is our turn as your children to take care of you. I don't want you to worry about anything the rest of your life."

Says Who?

With many of her words ringing in my ears, I left for Los Angeles to begin my rookie year in the National Football League.

I began my NFL career by setting a goal to play for 10 years in the league. At the time, the average player lasted only 3 1/2 years. To assist me in achieving that goal, I decided to identify those few individuals who had done what I was seeking to accomplish and to find out as much about them as I possibly could. I looked to seasoned veterans who had been around for 10 or 12 years, seeking to learn everything I could know about them.

I wanted to know about their lifestyle, practice habits, work ethic, their approach to the game, and their thought patterns. Most of all I wanted to know how they dealt with difficult circumstances in their lives, which challenged the achievement of their goals. I also wanted to know how they dealt with things not going as planned and how they dealt with negative comments from critics, which were not in alignment with their vision. But most of all, I wanted to know what really made them tick—what was really driving them.

While studying world-class athletes, I discovered that they approached life and the game of football in the same way I was conditioned by my Mom. I noticed that we shared similar thought patterns. Most of all, I noticed that many of them had to overcome difficult backgrounds and circumstances and deal with doubts expressed by others that could have knocked them off their goals.

I often wondered: "What drives these people?" I decided I was going to be on a constant search to find the answers. I felt that approach would better enable me to realize my goal of playing 10 years in the NFL.

After my first year in the National Football League, a defining moment occurred in my life. I went back to Texas to visit my Mom at her new home. As I was walking through the house, giving thanks for the small things that I always desired for her, like central heating and air conditioning, I walked into the dinning room and paused for a moment. When I looked through the dinning room window into the backyard, and on a cold mid-winter day, I noticed two large oak trees. Hanging between them was a clothes line, and on it were clothes, just as my Mom had envisioned when I was 13 years old.

The moment appeared to have caused time to stand still. For several seconds, I just stood in my tracks, staring at what was before my eyes. As I stared at the clothes on the line between the two oak trees, I reflected back on the obstacles and barriers that stood between my Mom's circumstance and her vision. I was curious to know how she remained focused on her vision, when it appeared the world was crashing in on her.

This prompted many different emotions and thoughts and even more questions: How did she do it without being knocked off her goal? How would things change in our lives based on our current situation? Why is that more people do not approach their lives in a similar manner? And, most of all, how could I help others to realize the inner-peace, self-satisfaction, and self-fulfillment I was experiencing at that moment?

Of all the things that have transpired in my life, the conversation I had with my Mom at age 13—when she shared the scriptures with me and confidently described her vision in the midst of what I personally saw as a world of chaos—helped develop my belief system. Witnessing the clothes hanging on the clothes line between the oak trees in my Mom's backyard just 10 years later inspired my life's mission.

Although part of her vision was realized through me, her son, I still wondered how she was able to stay true to her vision in life, despite the many overwhelming circumstances, obstacles, and barriers standing between her and her vision. When I inquired, she

replied simply: "I was placed here for you kids, to be the best mother I could be. My mission in life was to raise my kids to be the best that they can be."

Her comments echoed what she had said 10 years earlier when I was 13 years old. But then she added: "When I look back on my life, I feel immense joy for the special blessings that have come to me for being true to my purpose in life."

She continued, "When you look around and see what's going on in your life today, the only things that have changed—other than the fact that you're older and wiser—are your circumstances. And, just as it was easy to get all wrapped up in the adverse circumstances surrounding the way you grew up, it is just as easy to allow the success you are experiencing today to go to your head, and lose sight of how you got there."

Mothers keep you grounded. She then predicted: "Just as you had to face difficult circumstances and choices early in your life, you will face others as you get older. The key will be how you handle them."

Her comments caused me to have a greater desire to keep focused on my vision and mission in life and to be on a constant search for the most effective ways to realize my vision. It is a part of my mission to share with as many people as I can reach and touch this life-changing education.

Mother, I thank you, and hope to honor your blessed memory and to serve God by letting my light shine. Of all my life coaches, you were the first and the best.

Section 2
Patterns and Principles

Winners share certain patterns and principles of thought and behavior.

As I came into contact with more and more highly effective people, world-class athletes and other high-performance individuals, I observed that they were consistent in their ability to remain focused on their goals. Over the years, I have learned more about how they are able to accomplish this remarkable feat, in spite of encountering many things that could potentially knock them off of their goals and cause them to give up.

In this section, I will review what I have learned about success patterns and principles. I will share some of what I have learned about the patterns of winners, since many of us are susceptible to being knocked off our goals when we encounter life's challenges.

Chapter 5
Success Habits

Over the past 25 years, I've met many different individuals who have achieved an amazing amount of success, inner-peace and self-fulfillment in their lives. For some, the success came quickly and at an early age. For others, it came later in life.

Whether success came early or late, they appeared to have a unique ability to remain focused on their goals, despite encountering obstacles or barriers that could have potentially undermined their ability to achieve them. Their ability to stay focused on their goals, despite dealing with difficult challenges, better enabled them to utilize more of their potential, realize more of their dreams, and live the life they desire.

For some, their ability to persist and attain their goals seems to provide them with a certain level of inner-peace, self-satisfaction, and self-fulfillment that we desire in life for a job well done. They enjoyed the journey as much as the achievement of their goals.

As I came to know more high-performance people, I observed that they remained focused on their goals, despite encountering things that could knock them off of them. I wanted to know more about how they could do so, since so many of us can be more susceptible to being knocked off our goal when we encounter obstacles.

I also desired to identify the characteristics that enable this group to approach life the way they do. I wanted to identify what steps we can take to develop more of the wonderful characteristics

possessed by these highly effective people to enable us to remain focused on our goals, despite encountering obstacles or barriers that can potentially knock us off our goals.

In search of the answers, I studied the habit patterns of world-class athletes. As a professional football player, I considered this group near and dear to me. The better I understood and practiced the success strategies and tactics utilized by many of the greats of the game, the better I would position myself to achieve more of my goals in life and sports.

Five Common Characteristics

Most world-class athletes share five vital characteristics:

1. They share similar thought patterns. They have a certain way of thinking. They develop critical thinking skills based on their conditioning process. Many of them use positive thought patterns and certain success strategies to better enable them to remain focused on their goals when they encounter life's challenges.

2. They believe in a higher power. They remain faithful in their beliefs in difficult and tough times.

3. They are end-results oriented. They faithfully begin the process of goal attainment by keeping the end in mind. They begin with a clearly defined vision and purpose. Their goals have a purpose enhanced by their desire to improve their skill level daily; to be better today than yesterday, and better tomorrow than today.

4. They take daily incremental action steps. They develop a precise and disciplined plan of action and build a culture of discipline. They engage in disciplined thoughts, and they take disciplined incremental action steps.

5. When a problem arises, they first look to refocus on the desired target. In the midst of the storm, they lock on to the desired outcome and lock out the chaos that may be contributing to the storm.

How Is This Relevant to Me?

Often when I share my findings regarding world-class athletes and peak performers, people can't relate. They tend to think that members of this group possess special gifts, talents, or character traits; they do not see the relevance in their lives. Their perception is that these athletes have been blessed with special gifts and talents in a way that excludes all others in society. They feel that God had chosen the likes of Michael Jordan, Tiger Woods, and other world-class athletes to be destined for greatness in their chosen fields or professions—and that this somehow excludes them from attaining excellence. It's as if Jordan and Woods are members of an exclusive club—one to which they will never belong because they are just ordinary people.

During the latter part of my professional football career, I began comparing the psychological characteristics of some of the world's greatest performing athletes to peak performers in other professions. Part of my study was focused on highly effective real estate salespeople. My focus was to discover the basic differences in the thought processes between the two groups, but what I discovered was that both groups shared similar thought patterns.

Once again, when I shared my findings regarding the similarities between these groups, many people did not see the relevance to them, because they believed that the members of both groups had been blessed in a way that excluded them. In other words, they had some reason to justify why the athlete or peak-performing sales professional was performing at a level that was not available to them.

They felt limited, based on what they perceived to be things out of their control or beyond their means. As I reflected on this phenomenon, I became more interested in how we sometimes limit ourselves by the way we see, think, feel, and act. Our perception (how

we see things) is determined by the lens through which we see the world. And how we see things plays a vital role in how we think, feel, and act, and what we expect in life.

A Real-Word Example

For example, suppose you set a goal to study the stars in our galaxy, and you begin by going out on a clear night. You may witness many of the stars in the sky with your normal eyesight. After viewing the stars for a while with the naked eye, you may decide you would like to take a closer look at the stars. So, the next clear night, you go out with a pair of binoculars to improve the quality of your view of the stars.

On this night, you notice that the lens through which you look at the stars greatly improves the quality of your view of the stars. The lens of the binoculars enhances your ability to move closer to your goal of taking a closer look at the stars.

Unfortunately, when it comes to the lens through which we see the world, that is not always the case. The way we are conditioned to see and think plays a role in our perceptions. For example, suppose you desire to get an even closer look at the stars you are studying, and you take action. You seek out a friend, family member, or coworker who might assist you in achieving your goal.

Suppose you contact a coworker who collects various types of reading glasses, colored glasses, 3-D glasses, binoculars, microscopes, telescopes and other instruments with strong lens and a built-in filtering system. In fact, you know your friend has precisely what you are looking for to help you accomplish your goal. So you make your request: "I would like to borrow a pair of the strongest lens you have in your collection."

Suppose further that your friend knows you very well. You've known each other for years. He knows your likes and dislikes, strengths and weaknesses, and he's delighted to help you out. He responds by saying, "Sure, I'll bring them to work tomorrow and give them to you at that time."

Having enjoyed the astronomy experience you've had thus far, you can hardly wait for the next time you observe the stars. You get to work and greet your friend, who politely provides you with the strongest *micro*-scope in his collection. You say to him, "Thanks for the lens, but that's not what I'm looking for."

He replies by saying, "But you asked for the strongest set of lens in my collection, and that's what I'm providing you."

Many of us may find ourselves in a similar situation and later wonder, "What happened? Where did we go wrong?" Well, you can start with the lens with which we see the world and how we see things based on the way we've been conditioned.

No matter how great his desire to help you achieve your goal, if your friend has you looking through the wrong set of lens, he may unintentionally knock you off your goal. Even though you now have the strongest set of lens available to assist you in achieving your goal, you may only experience disappointment after disappointment, frustration after frustration. No matter, how hard you try or how much you believe in the equipment you have, your ability to be effective in achieving your goals is greatly affected by the lens with which your friend provided you to achieve your goal.

We have a natural filtering system that enables us to filter things through our senses of touch, smell, taste, hearing, and sight. The process is affected by our past experiences and by the authority figures in our lives. We forever perceive the world around us based on how we have been conditioned to think.

As you seek to know what viable steps you may take to develop the characteristics of highly effective people, I encourage you to become

more aware of how perceptions are formed, how they affect how you see the world, and how they govern the way you think and act.

To remain focused on your goals and utilize more of your potential, I also encourage you to become more aware of the role conditioning plays in the formation of your perceptions. The beliefs, habits, attitudes, and expectations you hold today are based on the way you have been conditioned to think.

If you and I are to remain focused on our goals in the midst of a storm and to grow and utilize more of our potential, we must continually assess why we see things, believe things, and do things the way we do. We must also be aware that "how we see the world" affects how we interpret the world.

Chapter 6
Beyond Quick Fix

Indeed, *how* we see the problem may be the problem.

People are often intrigued when they see good things happening in the lives of others whose lives are grounded on solid principles. They admire the character traits possessed by these individuals.

Many of the people who are thus intrigued may be experiencing a situation they are seeking to change or avoid for themselves, and their immediate reaction may be to appeal to someone: "Teach me how you do what you do in your life." What they may be saying is this: "Provide me with some magic formula that will solve all the problems in my life."

They seek to sort out people who will provide them with the techniques that meet their immediate needs. And, at least for a short period of time, they work at these prescribed methods. But after a while, they usually revert back to the situation they found themselves in. Once the process evaporates, they move on to the next quick fix, never really seeking to address the underlining issues that may be causing the problem.

Once I worked with a group of middle school principals. One of them shared a story about the problem he was having with one of the teachers in a particular classroom. After considerable consideration, he made a decision to move the teacher from one class to another. Soon, the same problem the teacher was experiencing in the previous classroom started to show up in the new classroom because the underlying problem was never addressed or dealt with. It was simply moved from one classroom to the next, and after a while, it reappeared. The change of classroom was just a quick fix, a band-aid placed on a symptom, without addressing the underlying problem. The more you try to solve the problem with a quick-fix, the more you contribute to the underlying problem.

Signs of the Quick Fix

At World Class Coaches, we see and hear the quick-fix approach often in the form of people sharing some of the following with us:

"I've attended time management seminars and training classes and they've helped some, but I feel like I'm under pressure all the time. There's never enough time to get all the things I have to get done, and still there's so much more I never get around to. I just don't feel like I'm living the life I desire to live."

"My (husband or wife) never listens to me. I tell (him or her) what I want, but they never listen. Everything seems to always fall on my shoulders. I try to communicate this point to (him or her), but I can never get them to listen. I can't count on them for anything. If I don't do it myself, it won't get done; yet, I have all these things to do, and no one to help me do them."

"I know I need to lose weight. I've tried several different diets, but none of them seem to be the right one for me. I set goals in this area of my life and things go well for me for a while, and then it just seems I lose steam and things fizzle out for me. I seem to have difficulty holding myself accountable."

"I have a desire to take my business to the next level, but I seem to be stuck. I've tried several different coaching programs; however, they don't seem to work for me. In some cases, I even changed coaches in an effort to find a coach to fit my personality, but on each occasion, it just did not work out for me."

After reviewing these statements, I concluded that these people may be looking for the answers in all the wrong places. They are looking for the next time-management seminar, magic-diet formula, motivational speech, or training program that will provide them with the answers.

Perhaps getting more things done during the day is not the answer. Will getting more things done make a difference, or, will it just add to a life that is already out of control? Could there be an underlying issue that may need to be identified and addressed in order to move from where you are today to where you desire to be? You may be looking for all the solutions outside of you, when the answers may reside inside you.

Again, when a problem arises, world-class athletes first look to refocus on the target they are shooting for. In the midst of the storm, they lock on to the desired outcome and lock out the chaos that may be contributing to the storm. With focus and the desired outcome in mind, they look inside and ask themselves, "What can I do to resolve this problem." They rely heavily on the guidance of their coach or other available resources to assist them in achieving their goals; however, they look for resolution of the problem from the inside out, starting first with proper alignment of their beliefs, habits, attitudes, and expectations with their vision, mission, and values.

When you are seeking to identify the problem or the solution for the problem, I encourage you to consider the possibility that the problem may not be in the classroom or with someone else—it may be somewhere inside of you. The way you have been conditioned to think affects how you see things. Your perception of the world and your expectations as a result of how you see things may be part of the problem. You, too, may be looking for answers in all the wrong places.

Chapter 7
Principles of Personal Growth

Many people in the world today promise that there is some quick-and-easy way to achieve personal effectiveness and quality of life, without taking small incremental steps.

But, I assure you that there are no magic wands or potions available to provide you with the quality of life you desire. You must go through the natural process of growth and development that makes it possible.

Many people may knowingly or unknowingly seek a "quick fix." They are looking for success without paying the price. At times, it might even appear to work; however, their success may be short-lived and based on a shaky platform.

Natural Growth Process

In all phases of our life, there are incremental stages in the natural process of growth and development. Children first learn to roll-over before they learn to crawl. They learn to walk before they learn to run. Personal growth and development is a natural process. Each step is important to the next step, and each step takes time.

This process applies to all forms of growth and development, whether it be communicating effectively as a salesperson or building a business. Although we know this to be true, sometimes we may seek to take a shortcut in the process of growth and development, expecting to skip some of the vital steps in an effort to save time and effort; however, we still hope to achieve the desired result.

The question is, "What happens if you try to shortcut this natural process?" Well, suppose you are an average bowler; however, you lead your friends to believe that you are a world-class bowler. One day you find yourself in a professional bowler's tournament. How would you expect to perform?

The answer is fairly obvious. To become a professional bowler— or to have a successful relationship, marriage, sports team, or company—you must go through a natural process of growth and development to achieve the desired outcome you seek. Any attempt to shortcut this process can lead to disappointment or frustrations.

Life is a journey. Like a trip you may desire to take, the first leg of the journey is to take the first step, then the second, the third, and so forth. The trip can only be completed by taking one step at a time.

Where Do You Stand Today?

Determining where you stand today in current reality is an important part of the process of traveling from where you are today to where you desire to be. Unless you know where you are today, you can't figure out what next step to take as part of the natural process of moving to the next level. This process appears to be fairly obvious in any sport, since it is almost impossible to hide as an average performer in a professional tournament; however, this may not be the case in other areas of our life.

For example, to be a highly effective salesperson, you need to develop a solid set of communication and listening skills and apply those skills when you need them the most. If you lack these human relations skills, because of the way you've been conditioned to think, this weakness may get in the way of your ability to take the necessary steps to realize the desired results you seek.

Our current level of development is fairly obvious as a bowler participating in a professional bowling tournament, where it's almost impossible to pretend. But it is not as obvious in the development of character traits and social competencies. Often, we can "pretend" or "fake it" in the presence of others and get away with it. Sometimes, we can even deceive ourselves; but deep inside, we know the real truth about who we are, and the strengths and insecurities we possess.

Many people in all sectors of society, in all walks of life, and at all levels of the social-economic scale often try to shortcut this natural process. Some go to seminar after seminar in search of the shortcut. Others look for external sources, seeking to identify the quick fix. Yet others seek to hide behind material things or job, title, position, or some form of status in search of the shortcut to get where they desire. When these methods don't work, they sometimes blame others. Or they look for other techniques outside of them that often ignore the natural principles and processes of growth and development.

Chapter 8
Weathering the Storm

Life is like a movie! When we think of a great movie, we often think of the plot and characters. It may be a love story, suspenseful drama, a mystery, fantasy, or real-life adventure that makes it a good movie. If you were to remove the plot, it would take away the appeal of the movie.

Life stories are often told through movies. That is why we see so many true stories on TV that become popular movies. We watch them to see how the characters deal with the challenges they encounter in life; how they handle things when a storm hits.

When watching a movie, we find these tests and trials appealing. In fact, if the movie lacked suspense, mystery, romance or adventure, we would not find the movie very appealing.

Think of your favorite movie and write down the name under number 1 on a piece of paper numbered 1 through 3. For number 2, write down why you enjoyed this movie. Now, for number 3, write down the plot of the movie. Typically, your responses to numbers 2 and 3 are similar. The plot is one of the reasons you like the movie

As you journey through life, your life will be filled with suspenseful, mysterious, and adventurous moments. These moments will come in the form of circumstances, things not going as planned, or comments you hear from others which are not in alignment with your vision. These circumstances create storms in your life. They bring chaos, suspense, mystery, adventure, drama, and the need to perform under pressure. How faithful you remain while in the midst of the storm will determine how well you remain focused on your goals.

Stormy Weather

You will find that it is easier to remain faithful and focused on your goals when the weather conditions reflect pleasant, sunny skies and 72 degrees outside. However, one key to remaining focused on your goals is to remain focused and faithful when you're caught in a storm.

SUNNY	SUNNY	CLOUDY	CLOUDY	CLOUDY
72 Degrees	100 Degrees	80 Degrees	Raining	Hurricane
Pleasant	Heat	Humidity	Storm	Panic

You may never know the depth of your faith or what you are made of on the inside until you find yourself in the midst of a storm. You may never know, unless you are put to the test. How you react in that moment, when the game is on the line, will provide you and those around you with a glimpse of who you see yourself to be on the inside and the depth of your faith. This is when you get a sneak preview of your subconscious beliefs.

When you find yourself in the midst of the storm, your deep-seated beliefs and true character traits rise to the surface. This is when you learn whether you believe in who you say you are as a person, or whether you are pretending to be someone or something on the outside you're not on the inside. This is when you learn what type of movie you are making. It is also where the superstars are made, or where people are labeled as "not able to handle the pressure." This is where the likes of Michael Jordan, Tiger Woods, Joe

Montana, John Elway and many other great sports legends have made their name. They do so by remaining faithful and focused on executing their plan of action while in the storm.

High Performance

Late in my professional football career I recall having a conversation with one of my mentors, Lou Tice, Co-Founder and President of The Pacific Institute. We talked about the high level of performance and achievement I had become accustomed to as a professional athlete and the fact that so many other individuals I was involved with daily were used to performing at the same high level.

He and I talked about the fact that although we had become accustomed to consistently performing at such a high level in sports, we did so in a natural and free-flowing way, even under pressure. We expected it of ourselves, and others expected of us. When we performed at a high level, we felt a real sense of inner-peace, self-satisfaction and self-fulfillment.

At this point, the focus of the conversation shifted to why more people in other chosen fields or professions often fail to utilize more of their God-given potential and fall short of realizing their goals to make a difference in society.

Lou said, "We all have dreams. We all want to believe deep down inside that we can touch others in a special way and make the world a better place to live."

I listened intently as he stated, "At one time in our lives, we all dream about a certain quality of life we desire and deserve. Yet for many of us, those dreams have become so covered in the challenges, frustrations, and routines of daily life that we no longer even make an effort to accomplish them. For many individuals, the dream has dissipated or died; and with it, so has the will to pursue their goals.

Says Who?

"We all encounter rocks in the road while pursuing our goals and dreams," he said. "These obstacles or barriers can come in many different forms, shapes, and sizes. For many people, life's tests can cause them to lose that sense of certainty that creates a winner's edge. As a world-class athlete, you encountered these same daily challenges in life; however, you managed to consistently find your way around the rocks in the road when they appeared, without having them affect your winner's edge. You will encounter many obstacles as you pursue your mission and vision in life. We all encounter them! How well you find your way around, over, or through the rocks in the road when you encounter them will determine to what degree you realize your mission and vision."

The Key: How We Cope

At this point of the conversation, I had a revelation, which has had a life-long impact on me. Regardless of who we are, where we come from, what social-economic level we fall on, or our chosen field or profession, we all encounter storms in our lives or rocks in the road that can get in the way of us utilizing more of our God-given potential and realizing the quality of life we desire. The key will be how effectively we deal with them when we encounter them.

In other words, you are no different than anyone else; we all encounter storms in our lives or obstacles or barriers in the road as we journey through life. These tests or nuisances either cause chaos in your life and knock you off your goal, or you learn how to effectively deal with them.

For some people, the obstacles may be the size of a pebble. For others they are the size of a boulder; and for others, these challenges are the size of mountains. The question I have for you is, "If you must encounter a rock in the road while pursuing your goals, which would you prefer it to be—the size of a mountain, boulder, or a pebble?"

I believe that not only is there a God but also that God does not place limitations on us. We either place them on ourselves, or we allow others to place them on us.

Section 3
Begin with the End in Mind (Vision)

In a sense, we are traveling through life without a clearly defined final destination or a viable flight plan if we are living from day to day without a purpose in life and a crystal clear vision. Living life without a purpose or vision only leads to chaos, frustration, and failure.

In this section, you will learn what you can do now to change the rest of your life.

Chapter 9
Identify What Makes You Tick

Suppose that you have been planning a vacation for several months. The time has finally arrived for you and your family to take that long-awaited trip to the desired destination. The only thing standing between you and the time of your life is the flight to one of your favorite places in the world.

You arrive at the airport in plenty of time to assure you're on time to catch a flight you booked four months ago. Once aboard the plane, you find yourself sitting on the runway, waiting for the plane to take off, when the pilot announces to the passengers they have not been given a destination for the flight, nor a flight plan to that destination.

So, there you sit on a plane full of jet fuel, with a flight crew, but without a specific target. How comfortable would you feel aboard the plane if the pilot decided to take off without having a specific destination for the flight or a flight plan to get you there? Imagine taking off without having a specific destination or flight plan. Without this detail, what basis would he use to make decisions once airborne? Without a purpose and a clear vision, what basis would you use to make daily decisions in life?

By nature, we are goal oriented. We operate and perform better when we begin with the end in mind. As human beings, we need a clear picture or target to move toward in life. We need a purpose and vision. If for some reason we are traveling through life without them, we are likely being driven by conditions and conditioning, by forces that can easily be affected by environmental influences and knock us off our goal.

Three Clocks

One day while working in my office, I noticed that each of the three different clocks in the office indicated a different time of the day. Knowing that there's one right time of the day, adjusted for the time zone we live in, I reflected for a moment on what makes each clock tick. I was interested in why each displayed a different time, because I had recently reset two of the clocks to the correct time.

As I contemplated what may be causing the discrepancy in time, I focused on the power source for each clock. I noticed that two of the three clocks were powered by batteries only, while the third one received its power from an electrical power source. Although each showed a different time, each had some source of power.

While assessing the power source of each clock, I thought of a fourth clock—one which I relied on heavily—the one associated with my cell phone. Although powered by a battery, my cell phone clock was very reliable. When I compared its time with that of the other three clocks, I noted that it had the same time as the clock powered by an electrical power source. I determined that these two clocks had the correct time of day.

What was curious to me was that the two clocks that showed the incorrect time were also powered by batteries. Whether it was the age of the batteries or some other reason, something had affected what made those clocks tick and altered their ability to perform properly.

I find these clocks to be apt metaphors for how we operate as human beings. As with the clocks, some power source affects our ability to be the best we can be.

For each of us, something or someone is guiding, directing, or controlling us in life. Right now you may be driven by pressure from a circumstance, by a deadline you're facing, or by a problem in your life. Or you may be driven by fears or a subconscious belief you hold.

Six Poor Power Sources

Hundreds of circumstances, conditions, or emotions can drive your life. Some are positive; others are negative. The following six power sources are usually negative:

1. Fear. Some people are driven by fear. Several different factors may contribute to a person's fears. These could be the result of growing up in a tightly controlled home with unrealistic expectations, a failed marriage, or failed business experience. Regardless of the cause, fear-driven people often miss out on great opportunities, because they are afraid to venture outside of their comfort zone. They usually seek to avoid risks by remaining where they feel most comfortable. Fear is a self-imposed prison that prevents you from utilizing more of your God-given potential and realizing more of your goals.

2. Anger. Some people are driven by resentment and anger. They experience hurt or pain as a result of others or circumstances in their life, and they hold on to them, instead of releasing them through forgiveness. They play their hurt and pain over and over in their mind. Some resentment-driven people "clam up" and internalize their anger, while others "blow up" and explode their anger onto others. Both can affect your ability to utilize more of your potential, and they can knock you off your goal.

3. Guilt. Some people are driven by guilt; they allow their past to control their future. They often punish themselves by sabotaging their own success. They spend their time running from regrets and

feeling sorry for themselves. People who live with guilt often find themselves wandering through life without a sense of direction.

4. *Need for Approval.* Some people are driven by the need for approval from others. In fact, they may go through life still trying to earn the approval of their parents. Others allow the expectations of their spouse, children, friends, co-workers, or peer pressure to control their lives. They're always worried about what someone else may say or think about them. Being controlled by the thoughts and opinions of others can greatly contribute to your failure to utilize more of your God-given potential and can knock you squarely off your goals.

5. *Need to Please.* Some people are driven by the need to please everyone. They have a need to be all things to all people. They are controlled by the inability to say no! They often find themselves spread so thin that they have difficulty focusing on any one thing long enough to complete the task. It's impossible to be all things to all people and to do everything people want you to do. Being controlled by the need to be all things to all people is a sure way to find yourself traveling through life with a lot of undue pressure and unnecessary stress.

6. *Possessions*. Some people are driven by material possessions. They have the misconception that the more things they have, the happier they'll be. They think that the more they have, the more important they'll be. They are driven by a label or a title. They have the feeling that their status will bring them more security, self-fulfillment and peace. Their self-worth is wrapped up in a name, title, home, neighborhood, or car. People who are driven by material possessions are usually always chasing more, thinking that more will bring them the inner-peace, self-satisfaction, and self-fulfillment they desire in life. That's not the case! Material possessions are temporary. They can be lost instantly through a variety of uncontrollable circumstances.

One Sure Power Source

There is one power source you can count on to keep you on goal.

7. Purpose. Some people are driven by a purpose in life. There are great benefits to living a purpose-driven life. Knowing your purpose gives you meaning in your life. It provides you with focus, simplicity, and motivation. Having a purpose provides you with a mission in life; it is what makes you tick. It becomes the standard you use to determine which activities are essential to assisting you in fulfilling your mission in life. It's the foundation on which you build and decide where you spend your time and how you use your resources. It's the power source that drives you in life.

People who live their lives without a clear purpose and mission usually try to be all things to all people. They tend to go through life making decisions based on circumstances, peer pressure, or comments they hear from others, all of which can potentially knock them off their goal. Often they try to take on more than they can handle at the time, which leads to undue pressure and stress and a life full of conflicts. That's because without a purpose in life, you have no foundation by which to make effective decisions regarding where you spend your time and how you utilize your resources.

Many people go through life without direction and focus. They are looking for security in all the wrong places; they are driven by factors outside of them. This often leads to frustration after frustration and living an unfulfilled life. Living a purpose-driven life can lead to a simpler, saner lifestyle.

Chapter 10
Live a Purpose-Driven Life

Have you ever asked yourself, "Why am I here on earth?" When I observe highly effective people, regardless of their chosen field or profession, one thing I notice about many of them is that they appear to be driven by something. Many feel they have a compelling reason for their existence—a purpose in life. They pursue a mission and vision in life with love and passion. It is what makes them tick.

When I think of my Mom, I often think of her comments, "I was placed here to raise my kids to be the best that they can be. That is my purpose in life. That's why God put me here." My Mom's approach to life was one of total selflessness.

In observing highly effective people, I find it interesting that for many of them, their purpose in life involves serving, helping, or entertaining others. They create an economic vehicle or identify a way to serve or help others in need or entertain others to the best of their abilities. And they manage to stay true to their purpose, even during the storms. The better they are at helping others meet their needs or achieving their goals, the more benefits and blessings appear to flow their way.

Whether you take the Mother Teresa approach of selflessness in helping people in need or the Bill Gates approach of identifying and fulfilling a need in society, staying true to your purpose will enable you to make a difference in society.

Says Who?

Although many high-performance individuals acquire a great deal of wealth, it is not necessarily the money that they are pursuing. What drives them, what makes them tick, is fulfilling their life's purpose or realizing their vision. With this approach, financial rewards appear to flow their way.

Professional athletes, entertainers, and top sales professionals are among the most gifted and talented people—and among the highest paid people—for having their light shine the brightest in their chosen field. The better they perform and the more consistent they are with their performance, the better they are compensated. However, it's rarely the money that's driving them; it's about being the best they can be. It's also about making a difference. With this approach, financial rewards are usually abundant.

Each of us is blessed in our own special way. You have your own set of special gifts and talents. There's no one else like you on the face of this earth.

With so many of us living our lives with a lack of direction and motivation, I often ask myself, "What's the difference between someone like Oprah Winfrey, Tiger Woods, and many other high-performance individuals and those individuals who find themselves wandering aimlessly through life?"

Well, peak performers represent a certain portion of the population who have identified their purpose in life and created a vision to support that purpose. They have identified a vehicle and developed the skills in their chosen field to achieve their mission and vision in life. For them, simply being the best that they can be, regardless of their circumstances, is part of what makes them tick. The better they perform, the more special blessings appear to flow their way. They're truly making a difference in society.

If you are among those people who are living life without direction and focus, I encourage you to listen to what Lou Tice has said: "At one time in our lives, we all dream about a certain quality of life we desire and deserve. And yet, for many of us, those dreams have become so covered in the challenges, frustrations, and routines of daily life, that we no longer even make an effort to achieve them. For many individuals, the dream has dissipated and died; and with it, so has the will to pursue their goals."

I hear Lou loud and clear. However, Mother Teresa never gave up on her dreams, although she encountered many challenges and difficulties in pursuing her mission in life. And I can't imagine Bill Gates, Oprah Winfrey, Michael Jordan, Tiger Woods, or the portion of the population they represent letting their dreams dissipate and die or losing their will to pursue their mission in life.

What enables world-class athletes and other high-performance individuals to remain focused on their goals, while others are easily knocked off of theirs? Part of the answer can be found in their ability to live a purpose-driven life.

Chapter 11
Establish a Clear Vision

From my experience in coaching and training thousands of individuals, I can attest that those who have a clear purpose and vision approach life with more love and passion. They seem to consistently be on a mission in life. Those who lack a clear vision often struggle with a lack of meaning and direction. Some even feel like a failure.

One of my fears during my professional football career was wondering if I could find something to replace sports in my life after retirement—something I could pursue with the same love and passion. I was not really concerned about finding something to do in life, because I knew several options would be available to me. What I was most concerned about was finding something that I could pursue with the same love and passion with which I pursued sports. Well, I found it in the World Class Coaches' vision and mission! It's part of what drives me now!

One thing I learned from elite coaches in the sports world is that they have a unique ability to take a group of individuals from various backgrounds and all walks of life, bring them together, and create a powerful team vision and mission. They do so with people from different beliefs, habits, and attitudes; people with huge egos and personalities who are paid millions of dollars for their athletic talents. Somehow they are able to keep the team focused on their goals and vision, despite their circumstances, things not going as planned for them, or comments they hear from others. Getting the most out of the people they coach is what drives many of them.

Why are you here on earth? What drives you? What makes you tick? What is your mission and vision in life?

I invite you to think seriously about these questions because the answers are critical to your future. Your vision and mission in life are the guiding forces behind the goals you set. They give meaning to your existence.

Having a crystal-clear vision is an important part of creating direction and motivation in your life. It provides a target for you to aim at to fulfill your purpose.

Vision: What you really want in life.

You determine your vision by asking yourself: "What do I really want in life?"

Without a purpose and vision, you tend to drift through life and be controlled by external drivers, ranging from fear to resentment, anger, material possessions, the need to please others, or some other environmental influence. With a clearly defined purpose, you are better able to make choices and decisions that support your vision in life.

For many people, living life without a vision and goals leads to chaos, frustration, and failure. After all, just imagine having the pilot take off without a specific destination or flight plan. Without this vision, what basis would the pilot use to make decisions once airborne? If you fail to establish a crystal-clear vision and goals, you have no basis for making daily decisions in life.

Your purpose in life is like the rudder on a ship—it provides you direction in life. It ensures that the results you are seeking are aligned with your vision. It helps you determine your priorities in life. Your mission ensures that you arrive at your intended destination, and that the quality of the journey is just as important as achieving the goal.

We all need goals to move toward—a target to aim for in life. We are built to have something pulling at us from the future. We seem to thrive when we have direction, something we are striving for, a mission in life. We can develop a sense of hopelessness when we lose that sense of direction. We do so because there's nothing really important to us. If you're going to live life to the fullest and find that inner-peace, self-satisfaction and self-fulfillment you desire in life, you not only need goals and a mission, you also need meaning and a purpose.

In other words, setting and achieving goals that simply enable you to own more things won't bring you lasting happiness and inner peace. Of course, financial success is important, but if the only reason you are working is so you can buy a new car every year or live in a fancy house that you fill with expensive furniture, you probably won't feel fulfilled. You'll never be able to buy enough or have enough. You'll keep raising the bar, having to own more and more, and still you'll feel that something is missing in your life.

So, I encourage you to know your purpose in life. Have a very clear vision and mission in life and believe strongly in what you are pursuing in life. Ask yourself why you want to succeed, why you chose your goals, and why you do the work you do. What is really important to you? It's important to ask yourself what's really driving you.

It's also important to remember that the ultimate goals you are striving to achieve must be properly aligned with the process you're using to achieve them. If you believe that your family is the most important thing in your life, but your job or career goals are keeping you too busy to spend much time with them, something is wrong. If your mission in life is to make the world a better place,

but you can't find time to support a good cause in your community, something is wrong.

I encourage you to set your goals so that they support and advance your purpose and mission in life. Identify all the key areas of your life and aim for balance. I encourage you to make sure you set goals in all the key areas that are important to you. Don't fall into the trap of thinking that you don't have enough time to live a balanced life. There's always time for the important things, because you're the one making decisions regarding where you spend your time in life.

As long as you are aware of your priorities, have a clear purpose in life and say no to those things that conflict with your vision, you can make solid daily decisions that enable you to remain focused on your goals.

Chapter 12
Writing Vision, Mission, and Value Statements

At each level of my sports career, the head football coach began the season by addressing the entire team and laying out the vision, mission, and goals. In an effort to create drive and focus for the team, the goals were put in writing and reviewed daily. This process assisted the team in the alignment of the team goals with its vision and mission. Proper alignment and clarity are two of the keys to establishing focus and direction in your life. Putting your vision, mission, and value statements in writing and reviewing them daily will assist you in creating clarity in your life. Proper alignment of your statements will assist you in creating more direction in your life.

Vision: What you really want in life

In writing your vision statement, keep in mind that it is a word picture of success for an individual or for an entity. It's a brief description of the desired outcome you're seeking, which you can easily visualize and understand. Your vision is the end result you're seeking when your mission is being accomplished. It is the picture for success towards which your goals and objectives are directed.

In writing your vision statement, describe your personal vision in life without placing any limitations on yourself. Often, when we set goals, we do so based on our perceived available resources to

achieve them. I encourage you to become a child again in writing your vision statement.

VISION
(What you really want in life)

Begin by asking yourself the question, "If resources were not a factor, what would my life look like?" "What would it look like in 5 years, in 10 years, and beyond?"

In providing your answers, describe those things you have always wanted to do, but for various reasons, have not done thus far in your life. Utilize your answers as a part of describing your vision. In a precise manner, describe what you really want in life.

If your mission does not support the achievement of your vision, one or the other needs to be adjusted. If your goals, objectives, and action plans are not leading you toward making the vision a reality, then your goals, objectives, or plans may not be focused on accomplishing the right mission.

Your Mission Statement

Your mission statement should describe your main purpose as an individual or entity. For an individual, it should describe your purpose in life, stated in terms of why God placed you here as an individual and your contribution to yourself, your family, or to society in general. For an entity, it should be a description of your chosen charter, stated in terms of your contribution to your customers or the market.

VISION
(What you really want in life)

MISSION

For an individual, the mission statement provides a sense of purpose and all the benefits that derive from having such sense of purpose. These include a higher sense of self-esteem, motivation, direction, and well-being.

For an entity, the mission statement should be broad enough in scope to include all the activities in which the entity wants to engage. It should also be narrow enough to eliminate activities that do not fit the charter. The latter is particularly useful for keeping the entity focused on its main business, while avoiding the pursuit of opportunities that do not fit the intentions of the founders or shareholders of the business.

In general, your mission statement should be short, memorable, and easy to describe. It's your answer to the question "what drives you?" For an entity, it's the answer that employees should be able to give in 30 seconds or less when asked "what does your company do?"

Every word in your mission statement should be carefully selected to accurately describe your purpose. If your mission statement is too long, or becomes too complicated or hard to describe, it can lead to a lack of clarity. Conversely, a mission statement that is easily understood is easier to engrain for faster responses, improved decision-making, judgment, priority-setting, a sharper focus, and concerted power in the activities you undertake.

Your Value Statement

Your value statement should reflect the principles that are most important to you as an individual or entity. They define your character and personality.

For individuals, your value statement should serve as the criteria for making decisions that often become life-changing. In business, stated values should serve as guidelines for making policy and other decisions and for setting priorities.

There are many good values, and selecting the few that are most important requires self-analysis and entity-analysis. In business, values are selected by owners or the management and leadership. Identifying the business values to emphasize is an opportunity to elicit positive responses from various audiences. Obviously, there are many values that are required for success in any field or profession.

VISION
(What you really want in life)

MISSION
VALUES

By selecting certain values in a value statement, you provide an opportunity to create a culture that has the characteristics that you, the management or ownership, believe will lead to success in the field of competition for shareholders, customers, employees, partners, and suppliers.

Values provide constraints on your vision and mission. They're also the underlying force or fuel that drives you as an individual or entity. They guide your decisions and actions. Values and the value statements can become a source of pride in the entity. Values are necessary to achieve high integrity and self-esteem.

Many values are required for success in any field or profession. Most are self-evident; however, some need an explanation.

In writing your value statement, consider that value statements are more fundamental than visions, missions, goals, and objectives. For an individual, your values can be the basis for making life-or-death decisions. They provide a basis for making many important decisions, including the selection of a spouse or career. Understanding values is essential to analyzing the causes of human action or inaction. In entities, values are often the real reasons a business exists.

Because various values are necessary for success, in writing your value statement, you may need to explain your selections in detail. Other explanations can be short enough to be included in the statement. It should be evident that the right values, properly prioritized, understood, supported and committed, can channel energy into extraordinary achievements. Aligning your vision, mission, and values in writing assists you to effectively deal with those things that can knock you off your goal.

START WHERE YOU ARE	PATTERNS AND PRINCIPLES	BEGIN WITH THE END IN MIND (VISION)	WHERE YOU STAND TODAY (CURRENT REALITY)	CLOSING THE GAP (VISION BECOMES REALITY)	KEEP ON COURSE	MAINTAIN FAITH IN THE STORM

Section 4
Where You Stand Today (Current Reality)

To align your mission and values with your vision and know what steps you can take to achieve your goals and realize more of your vision, I encourage you to determine where you stand today in current reality as it relates to your vision.

Chapter 13
Create a Gap in Your Life

Just as trying to live life without a designated target and a game plan to get you there can lead to chaos, seeking to achieve a goal without "a point of origin" can contribute to that chaos of living life without direction and focus.

Once you create a crystal clear vision and determine where you stand today in current reality as it relates to that vision, you create a gap between the two.

VISION
(What you really want in life)

MISSION
VALUES

(What you have gotten used to in life)
CURRENT REALITY

Your current reality is what you have gotten used to in life. Understanding the role this gap plays in your life is a prerequisite to taking steps to achieve your goals and realizing more of your vision. Once you create the gap between your vision and current reality in your life, you take a giant step toward creating more focus and direction in your life. You create an "area of focus" in your life.

By seeing the gap, you can better determine which steps you can take to achieve more of your goals and realize more of your vision.

And, you're better able to identify those things that can knock you off your goal.

Once you define a gap in your life and take steps to close it, you never actually close the gap, even though you may be achieving your goals. Once you start to close in on your vision, it moves up. That's because goal setting is an on-going process.

For example, suppose you set a goal to retire early at age 55, and you accomplish other goals that enable you to meet your retirement plans. Your focus then turns to goals and activities during your retirement years. Those activities may consist of traveling, spending time with your grandchildren, and scaling back your work schedule. Your focus shifts to what you want in life during retirement.

If you find yourself without a gap or if you let one gap close without creating another one, you may lose your motivation. One contributing element to your energy and drive involves the desire to close the gap between your vision and current reality. As human beings, our drive and energy come from having vividly defined lifetime goals to close the gap.

In sports, there's an old saying, "You're only as good as your last game." In spite of how well they have performed during the season or in the past, many athletes realize they are only as good as their last game (or last play). The elite performers approach each and every play as if it's their last one. World-class athletes and other peak performers become accustomed to this high standard.

One key step in establishing where you stand today in current reality is to know what you have gotten used to in life. As human beings, we are creatures of habit; we can get used to just about anything in life.

Many of the things in your life today, you have gotten used to as a part of your daily routine. The home you live in, the results you yield at work, the amount of income you earn, the car you drive, the way you treat yourself, the way you treat your spouse, the way you treat your kids are all things you have gotten used to in life. The quality of life you live today is something you've gotten used to in life.

If at times you feel as if you're the pilot at the controls of a plane that is airborne without a final destination or a flight plan to get you there, you have gotten used to living your life in that chaotic way. That is life in current reality for you today.

To create more clarity and focus in pursuing your vision, I encourage you to clearly identify those things you have gotten used to in life. This step will enable you to create a starting point for pursuing your vision and identify what changes you need to make and what steps you need to take to achieve your goals and realize your vision.

In writing your current reality statement, be concise. Describe those things you have gotten used to in life, both personally and professionally. Describe where you stand today financially. Describe the beliefs, habits, and attitudes you possess. Describe your skills and your strengths and weaknesses. Describe your life as you see it through your eyes today. This will enable you to create a clear and precise point of origin to begin moving toward your vision.

By having a solid starting point and a precise destination to shoot for in life, in the form of your vision, you are able to establish a precise game plan to close the gap—a game plan guided by a clearly defined mission in life and supported by solid values. When properly aligned, your vision, mission, and values provide a rock solid foundation to assist you in remaining focused on your goals, even when you find yourself in the storm.

Chapter 14
The Transformation Process

The successful transformation from where you stand today in current reality to where you desire to be with your vision is a process. There are certain things that must take place in order for you to successfully arrive at your destination. You need to make some decisions before you begin your journey and make other decisions during the transformation process.

As you take steps to close the gap between current reality and vision, you will make several decisions based on need and others based on personal preference, desire, or a goal you have set. Alignment of your vision, mission, and values with your needs, goals, and objective steps to realize your vision will play a vital role in the decisions you make as you go through this process.

Example: Buying a Home

For example, if you set a goal to purchase a home and save 10 percent of the desired purchase price for your down-payment, to achieve your goal, you would need to acquire financing for the remaining 90 percent of the purchase price of the home. It's important to understand the transformation process and the steps involved.

If your goal is to purchase a new home, and you only have 10 percent of the available resources to achieve your goal, that means you would need to find some other source, a lender, to assist you in completing your goal.

At this stage, you need to make several decisions, and with each decision, take a step. If you fail to take them, you compromise the attainment of your goal. For example, you need to decide which lender to use to acquire the necessary financing to complete the desired purchase. Once you decide on a preferred lender, you next need to decide when you will complete the lender's loan application, apply for the home loan, and select the desired loan program, based on your needs and goals. Again, if you don't take these steps, you compromise the transformation process from current reality to vision.

For some of us, we take some of these steps for granted. This type of mindset can lead to a lost of focus on the necessary steps required to close the gap. To successfully travel from current reality to vision, certain things must take place. Should these steps not be taken, you jeopardize your ability to realize your vision.

Needs and Goals

In the following illustration, notice that needs are on the left side of the pyramid and goals on the right. For every need in the transformation process, there must be a corresponding goal to meet that need. If you desire to purchase a new home with only 10 percent of the desired purchase price available to you, unless you set a goal to acquire the balance of the purchase price and fulfill that goal, you risk the achievement of your goal. You can have a goal (to live in a desired neighborhood) without having a need, but you can't have a need without having a corresponding goal. Notice the width of the base at current reality. As you meet more of the needs and achieve more of your goals, notice that needs and goals columns grow closer together as you near your vision. As you take the steps necessary to achieve your goals and remain focused on your goals, even in the midst of the storm, you position yourself to realize more of your vision.

VISION

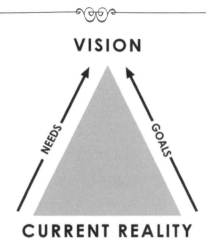

NEEDS

GOALS

CURRENT REALITY

During the transformation process, you may be faced with other decisions based on your preference, goals, or the value you place in certain areas. For example, if you were building a dream home as part of your vision, many of your decisions, such as number of bedrooms or bathrooms, would be the same, regardless of where you build the home. Other decisions might be driven more by a perceived need, such as making sure the home had a basement or storm cellar if you live in an area prone to tornadoes, or earthquake-proofed if you live in area prone to earthquakes.

In this case, the area where you live may possibly influence some of the decisions you make in building your home. Where you live may play a role in the final decision you make regarding whether you desire to have a basement or storm cellar in tornado country or a home that is earthquake-proof if you live in an area prone to earthquakes. In either case, the final decision is yours to make.

The alignment of your vision, mission, and values with your needs, goals, and objective steps are important to the transformation process from current reality to vision. If they are out of alignment, you may be more susceptible to being knocked off your goal, particularly in the midst of a storm.

VISION
(What you really want in life)

MISSION
VALUES

GOALS
NEEDS
OBJECTIVE STEPS

(What you have gotten used to in life)
CURRENT REALITY

Making Decisions

The *Says Who?* approach is to live life on an "I choose to," "I like it," "I love it," basis. In others words, there are no "I have to's" in life. You do not "have to," or "need to" do anything.

There are decisions you have to make in life, and your decisions will affect your ability to remain focused on your goals. If you feel you "have to" do things, you really don't! You do have choices and decisions to make. Should you choose "not to," or should something prevent you from making a decision, there are consequences to your actions.

For example, you may think that you "need to" or "have to" work; however, you do not. If you choose not to work, the consequences may prevent you from providing for your family, sending your kids to the college, or living the life you desire.

If you feel you are stuck on a dead-end path, you have a choice to make as well. You can choose to live your life on an "I have to" basis and remain on the path, or you can make a decision to pursue the life you truly desire. The transformation process from current reality to vision begins with a decision by you. One of the keys to remaining focused on your goals will be your ability to make logical and wise decisions during the transformation process when you encounter storms in your life. The journey is filled with important decisions to be made to cover the steps of the process.

Once you decide that you desire to transform from current reality to vision and meet the needs and achieve the goals to realize your vision, you face certain steps to assure that you are proactively traveling toward your destination or vision. Each step requires a decision and is considered a mini-goal—one that when achieved will enable you to move one step closer to meeting your needs, achieving your goals, and realizing your vision.

Example: Taking a Trip

Making the transformation process from current reality to vision is like taking a trip from Los Angeles, California, to New York, New York. To achieve your goal, certain steps must be taken to move from your point of origin to your destination.

The purpose behind the trip to New York will drive many of the decisions you make during the trip. If the purpose of the trip is for business and it requires you to be there at a certain time, that deadline may well influence your decision-making process regarding the method and route you take to your destination.

Once you make that decision, certain things need to take place in order to transform from point of origin to desired destination. For example, if you are traveling by plane, you would need to decide the date, time, and flight you desire to take to complete the trip. Once you make that decision, you need to purchase a ticket and make sure you arrive at the airport in time to catch the flight.

Although these steps must be taken to move toward your destination, you do not actually "have to" take them. However, should you fail to do so, you will suffer the consequences. For example,

failure to purchase or acquire an airline ticket would prevent you from traveling by plane. For each need, there must be a corresponding goal to meet that need in order to transform from current reality to vision. If you have a need that must be met to transform from current reality to vision, you must have a corresponding goal to meet that need, if you are to achieve your vision.

Many of your decisions would be based on your answers to certain questions about the purpose of the trip; other decisions would be based on who may be traveling with you and what sites you may desire to see along the way. These are important questions to be asked and answered, as your mission will be found in the purpose of the trip.

Again, the *Says Who?* approach suggests that you do not need to do anything in life. You have choices to make! There are consequences for your decisions; however, the decision is yours. The more effective you are in the decision-making process, the more you remain focused on your goals, even when you find yourself in a storm.

Another decision that will greatly affect the transformation from current reality to vision involves the economic vehicle you choose to utilize to realize your vision. A destination, without a sound plan and well-maintained vehicle to get you there can knock you off your goal.

Your Economic Vehicle

For many highly effective people, their purpose in life involves serving, helping, or entertaining others. They create or identify an economic vehicle to serve or help others in need, or entertain others to the best of their abilities, and they stay true to their purpose, even in a storm. The better they become at helping others meet their needs or achieve their goals, the more special blessings appear to flow their way.

For many of us, our economic vehicle is much like the automobile we drive to work each day. It serves as a means to get us from where we are today to where we desire to get in our life, our vision. Just as we need our car to get us to and from where we desire, we need our economic vehicle to serve the same purpose, as it relates to the transformation from current reality to our vision.

The economic vehicle can mean something different for each person. Some people may drive a $100,000 automobile, and someone else may drive a $20,000 automobile. For some people, their economic vehicle may be a 9 to 5 salary position, with benefits and holidays and weekends off. For others, their vehicle may be that of an independent contractor or business owner.

Although your economic vehicle plays a vital role in your life, it's a relatively small part when you look at the overall scope of your life. In the above illustration, notice the proportion of your economic vehicle in your life. Notice how small it is, as it relates to the scope of the illustration.

Says Who?

Although your economic vehicle represents a relatively small part of your life, it can knock you off your goal if you approach it casually. If you drive a six-cylinder automobile to work and one of the cylinders is not operating properly, it may cause your car to sputter along. Should two or more cylinders not operate properly, your car may break down completely.

How well you maintain your economic vehicle will determine how efficiently and effectively it runs, as well as the economic return you can expect to receive from it. Suppose, for example, that you are a self-employed person who has a goal to earn enough money to create a passive income stream for retirement. However, you have a habit of procrastinating when you should be conducting lead-generation activities. That poor behavioral pattern is like a dysfunctional cylinder. Sooner or later, it may cause your car to break down. If you fail to correct the behavioral pattern of inconsistent lead-generation activity, which is a vital part of your economic vehicle, it could knock you off your goal.

So, the better you grow personally and professionally, the better you will maintain your economic vehicle. The better maintained the vehicle you are driving to realize your vision, the better you stay true to your purpose, and the more difference you make in society. With a well-maintained economic vehicle, the better you remain focused on your goals in a storm.

Chapter 15
Things that Can Knock You Off Your Goal

During my NFL stay with the Los Angeles Rams, I recall a play-off game against the Washington Redskins, in Washington, D.C.

Our goal for the day was to defeat the Redskins and move one step closer to our ultimate goal of winning the Super Bowl. To achieve our primary goal of winning the Super Bowl, we needed to accomplish our goal for that day—to score more points than the Redskins. We needed to win the game.

Eric Dickerson, our star running back, broke free on what appeared to be a sure touchdown run of more than 65 yards. With Eric running in the open field with no player of the Redskins between him and the goal line, it appeared he would score. In fact, when he initially broke free of the line of scrimmage, there was no Redskins' player within five yards of him as he headed for the goal line and a touchdown.

As Eric crossed mid-field, Darrel Green, the Redskins' cornerback and one of the fastest men in the National Football League at the time, came out of nowhere and caught up with Eric from behind and tackled him before he could cross the goal line and score.

Eric and Darrell were opponents in the game. Eric's goal was to score a touchdown; Darrell's goal was to knock him off his goal of scoring the touchdown. Each player knew the rules of the game, and they were prepared to knock each other off their goal.

In the game of life, our opponents, those things that can knock

us off our goal, are not as obvious as they are in football. In fact, we may not even be aware of what they are or who they are, and yet they can knock us off our goal.

Three Primary Areas

Through the coaching process at World Class Coaches, we've discovered three primary areas where people are most susceptible to being knocked off their goal:

- Circumstances we find ourselves in;
- Things not going as planned in our lives;
- Comments we hear from others.

These things are not in alignment with our goals. These situations create storms in our lives whenever we encounter them. In fact, these three areas of our lives seem to play the role of Darrel Green in knocking Eric Dickerson off his goal to score a touchdown.

We all encounter hundreds of circumstances that can create a storm in our lives. Each circumstance brings about a different emotion within us, which causes us to react a certain way. If our reactions, decisions, or actions are not aligned with our vision, the storm can knock us off our goal.

We all have to deal with these three areas at some point in our lives. No one is immune. Highly effective people and high-performance individuals encounter them as well. These three areas contribute to the plot of the movie of our lives. Our responses to these three factors often determine whether the plot is a mystery, drama, comedy, or tragedy. Certainly some life events are more dramatic than others. Dramatic storms make movies appealing and our lives interesting.

But your life is not a movie, and you, by being proactive in your responses to the circumstances of your life, can actually write the script of your life. And if you invite God to be your co-author, the script of your life will read much better.

I believe there's a God. I also believe that God does not place limitations on any of us. We either place them on ourselves, or we allow others to place them on us.

It's not the storms you encounter in life that ultimately make the difference between success and failure, because we all encounter them—it's how you deal with the storms in your life and how well you remain focused on your goal.

It's not the circumstance you find yourself in today or the negative comments you hear from others that knock you off the goal; it's your reactions to them that may knock you off the goal. It's not the fact that things are not going as planned that knocks you off your goal, it's your reactions and decisions you make to things not going as planned that can knock you off your goal.

Our reactions to the storms in our lives are based on the way we have been conditioned to think, believe, and behave. Something is guiding, directing, or controlling us in life. These drivers are based in part on our subconscious beliefs.

Six Emotional Reactions

When we encounter a storm in life, we may react a certain way, based on our perception of what may have caused the storm or the circumstances surrounding it. In Chapter 9, we talked about *Six Poor Power Sources* that may affect your ability to remain focused on your goals. Based on our subconscious beliefs, the storm may cause us to emotionally react in a manner consistent with one of the potentially negative power sources.

Here are six common emotional reactions to the storms in our lives. Any one of these can potentially knock us off our goal.

Fear. Fear-driven people often miss out on great opportunities when they find themselves in storms, because they're afraid to venture outside of their comfort zone. They seek to avoid risks by remaining where they feel most comfortable. Fear is a self-imposed prison that can potentially knock you off your goal. Often it is in storms when many rewards are realized. It is also at that time when many fear-driven people retreat to the safe haven of their cocoon, seeking safety from the storm.

Anger. Some people carry resentment and anger around with them as a result of the storms in their lives. When another storm blows in, they either "clam up" and internalize their anger or "blow up" and explode their anger onto others. They lose focus of the goal they are pursuing and become more intent on revenge for what has taken place in their lives, rather than seek a solution or resolution to the problems contributing to the current storm. Their angry reactions to the storm, and the decisions they make, cause them to lose focus of the goal and knock them off their vision.

Guilt. Like people who carry resentment and anger around with them because of storms in their lives, guilt-driven people allow their past to control their future. They often look for storms in their lives, punishing themselves by sabotaging their success. They spend their time running from regrets and feeling sorry for themselves. During storms, people who live with guilt often wander through life without a sense of direction, and their lack of focus can knock them off their goals.

Need for approval. Some people go through life trying to earn the approval of everyone they come in contact with. They allow the expectations of others to control their lives. Some become paralyzed, waiting for the approval of someone else before they can move forward on their own. They're always worried about what someone else may say or think about them. They are controlled by the thoughts and opinions of others. Their needs, based on their beliefs, can greatly contribute to their failure to utilize more of their God-given potential during storms, and they can knock them squarely off their goals.

Need to please. Some people have a need to be all things to all people. They are controlled by the inability to say no! During storms, they often find themselves spread so thin that they have difficulty focusing on any one thing long enough to complete the task. Although spread thin, even in storms they still seek to please, when they should be seeking solutions to their problems. Being controlled by the need to be all things to all people can cause you to lose your focus and knock you off your goal.

Material possessions. Some people have the misconception that the more things they have, the more important they'll be or the happier they'll be. They think that their status will bring them more security, self-fulfillment, and peace. All of their self-worth appears to be wrapped up in a name, title, home, or car. People who are driven by material possessions are usually always chasing more, thinking that more will bring them the inner-peace, self-satisfaction, and self-fulfillment they desire in life. During storms, our material possessions can be taken away from us. They can be lost instantly in conditions and circumstances we can't control. Our focus on materials possessions for the wrong reasons can knock us off our goal.

Our beliefs, habits, attitudes, and expectations determine our reactions to the storms in our lives. If you feel you have been wronged by someone and you fail to forgive that person or yourself, then any time you are reminded of that situation, you may react in a resentful, angry, or guilty manner. And if you continue to react in this manner, these behavioral patterns will soon feel normal. They

will be what you get used to in life. If these behavioral patterns are out of alignment with your purpose and vision, they can potentially knock you off your goal.

Chapter 16
Who Are the Authority Figures in Your Life?

Have you ever wondered how you developed your beliefs and habitual behaviors?

Let me suggest that many of your core beliefs come from the authority figures in your life. And even though these people may possess the purest of intent when they try to help you or teach you, they can knock you off your goal.

How does this happen? It happens when they convey to you their point of view on what is in your best interest based on limited information or limited thinking, and their opinions are not in alignment with your goals. This process also plays a role in how you develop the beliefs you hold.

Parents and Children

Once, I served as a youth volunteer sports coach and closely observed the interactions between parents and their kids. Such interactions contribute to the development of the beliefs we hold today.

For example, in professional football, I learned five fundamentals that are vital to the success of any football team. As a youth football coach, I teach these five basics to the youth I work with: 1) tackle well, 2) be a sound blocker, 3) protect the football, 4) run full speed at all times, and 5) have fun playing the game. In addition, I have one basic rule for the team: "To be the best you can be."

The tenet to "run full speed" is an attempt to remove the hesitation from their play. Some kids have a tendency to hesitate before their every move, and one of the reasons for this hesitation is usually because the kids fear making a mistake and having their parents embarrass them by verbally communicating their displeasure in front of all their friends for not living up to their expectations.

So, these kids learn to seek approval from their parents for their performance. The parents unwittingly develop in their kids the need to please and the need for approval from others by showing or expressing their frustrations when their kid's performance falls short of their expectations. The kid might tell me, "Coach, nothing I do will ever please my dad."

If the parent continues to verbally react in a critical manner, the kid may feel that he is unable to live up to his parents' expectations and be conditioned to think and react a certain way. After a while, the kids develop beliefs and carry these with them for the rest of their lives, or until they decide to change them.

Some of the beliefs we hold today come from our parents or other authority figures expressing their displeasure of our performance during dance practices or soccer games. Children may be told by parents, authority figures, teachers, or relatives that they are "dumb," "can't get anything right," "can't draw," "aren't good at sports" or are "clumsy" over and over again. As they continue to hear these negative statements, they begin to lock-on to those limited or false beliefs—and then act on the basis of them.

Perceptions About Performance

Another way we can lock-on to a mistaken belief about ourselves may be how we perceive our performance in a particular situation. I recall an assignment given to a gifted and talented lady during our coaching. She was requested to assess the possible causes of her way of thinking. The purpose of the exercise was to identify factors that contribute to how she thinks. I thank her for allowing me to share the results of her assignment.

I can probably trace my insecurities back to the eighth grade. Here's what happened in Mrs. Jones's speech class: We were assigned to speak about any topic we wanted. I was fascinated with the construction of a suspension bridge near my home on Long Island, New York, so I chose that topic. I told the class that I was going to talk about how to build a suspension bridge.

Well, I left the assignment to the night before it was due, so I hurriedly pulled a few paragraphs out of the encyclopedia that described what a suspension bridge was, not how it was built. I gave my speech, and at the end, one kid raised his hand and asked, "But how do they build a suspension bridge?"

I was mortified! I still get nauseous thinking about that moment. I was so ill-prepared that I couldn't answer the boy's question.

I am convinced that experience made me such a thorough reporter, possibly even obsessive, years later. The fear of being seen as being unprepared or uninformed created an internal pressure to always "get it right." I would never be caught without the facts again. Fear has been one of the motivating factors in my broadcast career.

If you look back on your life, you might recall a situation where, whether you were prepared or not, you did not perform as well as expected, and someone called you on it. And you may have believed that you lacked the ability to perform as expected.

As a result, you now try to avoid repeating that same experience, and that avoidance tendency affects the way you think! You impose limitations on yourself—limitations that do not reflect your true God-given gifts and talents, but more accurately reflect how you've learned to think about yourself and those around you. You then become used to certain things in life—things that can knock you off your goal, if they are not in alignment with your vision, mission, and values.

For this reason, I encourage you to constantly assess why you may be thinking the way you're thinking today. If you're not realizing the results you are seeking, ask yourself, "What is holding me back from achieving my goals?"

In addition to limiting yourself based on your fear of not performing as expected, how else might you be limiting yourself in how you think? What might be some other limited beliefs that prevent you from realizing more of your God-given potential and achieving more of your goals? How might you be reaffirming those limited beliefs with how you talk to yourself?

How often do you say, "I'm a really shy person" or "I'm just not good at that" or "I can't afford that?" or "I can't do that?" These are examples of negative affirmations that some people use daily, without understanding the impact they have on their belief system and their performance.

I encourage you to become more aware of the strength of affirmations, statements of beliefs that you continually tell yourself. Your subconscious mind accepts what you affirm and works to carry it out for you. Your mind accepts a belief until you change it. Even a one-time affirmation by another person can have a huge impact on your behavior.

For example, at a marriage ceremony, the person conducting the wedding makes the following statement: "By the power vested in me, I pronounce you man and wife." And you affirm, "I do." With that affirmation, you go through a rite of passage and may change the way you behave to be aligned with the behavior of a married person.

Conversely, if the marriage goes bad, you go through another rite of passage—one conducted by a judge who states, "By the power vested in me, I dissolve this marriage." You accept, and with that, you now go out and act like a single person. Sacraments in religions are usually rites of passages with affirmations.

The world is full of rites of passage. When you graduate from college, you're awarded a diploma, which certifies that you are educated. After certification, you are expected to act the part. A doctor goes to medical school and, after fulfilling all the requirements to become a doctor, is granted a license to practice medicine. Yesterday, you were just a medical student, but today, after a rite of passage, you're a doctor. If you had a medical condition that required treatment, how comfortable would you feel having the medical student treat you, as opposed to someone with a medical license?

I encourage you to assess what enables someone not to be educated one day, and then receive a diploma and be educated the next day—to be a medical student one day and a doctor the next day. Without making light of the process it takes to become a doctor, think about what really transpires to cause the change in our belief system and expectations by which we live our lives. In each case, there is an authority figure who presides over a ceremony or certification process, which validates the rite of passage.

Off to See the Wizard

Many different authority figures bestow their beliefs upon us. Some of those people are good for us, and some are bad. If we believe their pronouncements to be true, we will act according to those beliefs.

Says Who?

In *The Wizard of Oz*, Dorothy and Toto were lost. Their goal was to get home to Kansas. In their search for home, they met a good witch who said, "You must go and see the Wizard of Oz. He has the power to help you." So off they went to see the Wizard.

Why did they go? They went because of their belief in the power of the Wizard and in all the wonderful things he could do with those powers. But when Dorothy, Toto, the Tin Man, the Scarecrow, and the Cowardly Lion found the Wizard, they learned that he was really a false Wizard. Still, they chose to believe what he had to say. So, he gave the Tin Man a heart, the Scarecrow a new brain, and the Cowardly Lion the courage he always wanted. He made the Tin Man's heart tick, and he gave the Cowardly Lion a medal for being brave. He gave the Scarecrow a diploma. "Now go and act smart," he told the Scarecrow, and to the Lion, he said, "You're no longer a coward; go forth and act brave." And they all chose to believe him. Such a powerful affirmation in a rite of passage can change you forever because it changes a belief about yourself.

Authority figures come in many types, shapes, and sizes; some are good, and some are bad. Some of them can assist you in remaining focused on your goals, and others can knock you off your goal by their affirmations, if you accept them.

For example, you may have heard someone say, "You have to know the right people to get one of those upper-management jobs, so it won't do you any good to apply." What about, "No one has ever done that before," or "It can't be done that way!" How about, "A woman has never held that position before."

These one-time affirmations from negative authority figures in your life can take away your brains, your heart, and your courage. They can rob you of your ability to utilize more of your God-given potential, and they can knock you off your goal.

Who are the authority figures in your life—perhaps your spouse, parents, friend, co-worker, coach, or mentor? Who are the authority figures in your company? Who declared them to be so? Are they a positive or negative authority figure, based on your vision, mission, and values in life? And how do you respond when you hear comments from them? Are the comments you hear from them in alignment with your goals?

I realize that you can't avoid coming in contact with negative authority figures in life. I also understand that you can't always control what someone may say to you, or a circumstance you may find yourself in; however, you can control your reaction to what is said to you, or your reaction to the circumstance.

Ask yourself, "Who are the authority figures I listen to? Are their views in alignment with my views on life and with my goals? Are they constructive or negative authority figures? And to what degree do I buy into their opinions?

I believe that when you are pursuing a solution to a problem or achievement of a goal, either the answer already exists or the path to attaining the goal is present. It's just that you may not see it at the moment. When a teacher prepares a student for an exam in school, the answer exists. The teacher's job is to help the student learn the answer.

The *Says Who?* approach is to constantly search for the answer to the problem or the path to the goal. It's a way of thinking! So, the next time a limiting thought enters your mind, ask yourself, "Says Who?" The next time someone makes a limiting comment to you, such as "You can't do it that way!" I encourage you to stop the negative way of thinking by asking, "Says who?" Ask yourself why you are thinking the way you're thinking as you proactively search for a better way to remain focused on your goals.

Section 5
Closing the Gap
(Vision Becomes Reality)

When you close the gap between vision and current reality, your vision becomes your reality. You become an option thinker. You unlock your mind and unleash your potential. You align your beliefs, habits, attitudes, and expectations with your vision. You lock-on to what you want to accomplish (your circle of focus) and lock-out other options. Ultimately, you accept personal accountability for your behavior and take proactive steps to close the gap between current reality and vision.

Chapter 17:
Adjust the Lens for Seeing the World

Have you ever wondered how two people can look at the same thing and see two different things? Why is it that "the truth" can seem so different to different people? How can two people try to accomplish the same thing, and it seems to be easy for one but difficult for the other?

We see this often in life. When it happens to us, we may blame others or ourselves if we don't achieve what we desire right away, or if we don't achieve it as fast as someone else does. At times we may think we're not smart enough or good enough to accomplish what we are seeking. This way of thinking can knock you off your goal.

I developed a vision to be a peak performance coach at a young age. My desires to coach expanded beyond the sports world. I felt I wanted to have a greater impact in society than just coaching sports, as helping others to be the best they can be is a part of my personal mission in life. It is a part of my mission to make a difference in society.

Equipped with a clear vision and mission in life, I shared my vision and mission in life with Lou Tice, who has spent a lifetime assisting others in meeting their needs and achieving their goals. Lou recommended that if I desired to fulfill more of my mission in life, it may serve me well to gain some valuable business experience in some other sector of society.

Although I clearly understood the significance of his suggestion,

Says Who?

I felt limited in my options to fulfill his recommendation, primarily because of how I viewed myself and the world around me; I saw myself as a professional athlete. My entire life was centered on being a pro football player. That is how I saw the world, and that is how I felt the world saw me.

Lou's recommendation to gain business experience in another area of my life, other than sports, caused me to evaluate the lens I was seeing the world through. If I were to realize my vision and mission in life, I would need to gain the business experience Lou suggested, which required me to explore viable options in alignment with my vision and mission in life. It also required me to adjust the set of lens through which I was seeing the world.

Through what lens are you seeing yourself, others, and the world? The lens you look through will determine how you see the world.

Option Thinking

The *Says Who?* approach is to be an option thinker; to think outside your current limitations. For this reason, I encourage you to be as creative and innovative as you desire to be to realize your vision; however, I encourage you to do so within the confinements of your vision, mission, and values in life.

This process will enable you to see the answers to the problems, or the way around the rocks in the road on your way to achieving your goals. It will enable you to see with more focus and clarity those options and opportunities when they appear while pursuing your goals.

Filters and Blind Spots

The *Says Who?* way of thinking is that the opportunities are present; we just may not have seen them yet. What might prevent you from seeing things as clearly as you desire when opportunities present themselves to you? One barrier is your natural filtering system—your senses.

You naturally filter things through your five senses of taste, sound, sight, touch, and smell. Based on how you've been conditioned and your life experiences, you see the world through a certain lens. Because of the way you've being conditioned to think and your filtering system, you've developed blind spots that prevent you from seeing the various options you may need to see to remain focused on your goals, although these options may be right in front of you.

How well you deal with blind spots will determine how well you remain focused on your goals. You may not even know that you have them. One way that you can recognize you have them is when you hear yourself saying, "This doesn't make any sense to me," or "I don't get it." This is how you can recognize a blind spot.

Blind Leading the Blind

Blind spots are serious shortcomings! Marriages often fail because partners have blind spots. Businesses often fail because their leaders have blind spots. Friendships often dissolve because of blind spots. No one is immune from having blind spots.

We have a blind spot whenever our senses lock out our environment. It's a process that causes us to see what we expect or want to see, hear what we want to hear, and think what we desire to think. "I've always done it that way." "I'll never be able to do it." This locking-on and locking-out process creates our blind spots.

Although we all have blind spots, world-class athletes, highly effective people, and high-performance individuals seem to have fewer ones than people who perform at a lower level. That's because they learn to adjust the lens they look through, as needed, to remain focused on their goals.

This was the case with my looking to take steps to gain the business experience Lou suggested. I had developed a blind spot in my life, based on the way I had been conditioned to think and the set of lens through which I viewed the world as a result of that conditioning. The blind spot had the capabilities of coming out of nowhere and knocking me off my goals, just as Darrel Green knocked Eric Dickerson off his goal.

Blind spots were not new to me; I was well aware of the possibility that they existed. I also took steps as a professional athlete to minimize their impact in my life. I did so by using the *Says Who?* approach of assessing why I may be thinking the way I am thinking, if my thoughts are out of alignment with my goals. I would ask, "Where did those beliefs come from?"

If I heard comments from someone else, which were not in alignment with my goals, I would not take them for face value. I would thoroughly assess them first to seek to determine, "Why are these people thinking the way they are thinking, and what are they basing their opinions on?"

As a professional athlete, it was a part of my approach to be on a constant search for a better way to accomplish my goals. Once I adjusted the lens through which I see the world, I could better see the possibility of gaining the business experience in some area of my life other than football. Prior to my seventh year in the NFL, I became a licensed real estate professional. Given my goal to play 10 years in the league, I would have three years to gain the business experience suggested by Lou Tice.

Highly effective people and high-performance individuals recognize that they may not see all that they need to see. They are analytical in their approach to life. They question those things that conflict with their beliefs or points of view in a positive and constructive manner as they search for the answers to their questions, or for means to realize their goals.

Seeing all that you need to see and eliminating your blind spots has little to do with how smart you are or how gifted or talented you are. But it has a lot to do with how you think, what you believe, and through what lens you look.

Lock On, Lock Out

If you're able to adjust the lens you see through, you may actually benefit from having blind spots. Setting a goal allows you to lock-on to that goal, and lock-out needless distractions. So, as you lock-on to a goal with clarity, you can focus intently on achieving the goal, while locking-out needless distractions. This focus enables you to deliberately lock-out those things that can knock you off your goal.

This is a tremendous advantage to have. Be careful, however, as one of your greatest strengths could become one of your most challenging weaknesses. Your ability to focus and concentrate, to lock-on to a goal or a way of doing something, could cause you to overlook valuable options, which may be available to assist you in realizing your goals. This is due, in part, because of your beliefs and the lens through which you see the world.

Most people leave out important parts of reality because they are conditioned to think a certain way and see a certain way. If you become so locked-on to an idea or approach, you can completely lock-out another potentially more creative or productive option.

Once you lock-on to an opinion, belief or attitude about yourself or someone else, it becomes difficult to see or understand things that may conflict with your beliefs. You become less aware, perhaps com-

pletely unaware of an alternative way of seeing things.

This blindness can make change and flexibility difficult, because you tend to think about one thing at a time. You tend to receive only information that will validate your point of view. The key is to know when to lock-on and when to lock-out.

So, I encourage you to adjust the lens you see the world through and become an option thinker—someone who is searching for a better, more effective way of realizing your goals and living the life you desire. This ability will enable you to remain focused on your goals, even in the midst of the storm.

Chapter 18
Unlock Your Mind, Unleash Your Potential

As President of World Class Coaches, I meet individuals from all walks of life and all levels of the social-economic scale who are performing at the same high level in their chosen fields or professions as world-class athletes. This is due in part to the development of critical thinking skills by many of these high-performance individuals and the proper alignment of their behavioral patterns with their mission and vision in life.

Once you determine your purpose in life and define your vision and mission, I encourage you to take steps to properly align your beliefs, habits, attitudes, and expectations with your goals. If properly aligned, attainment of your goals will lead to achievement of your mission and vision in life.

Start with Beliefs

I recommend that you first assess for proper alignment between your beliefs and your vision, mission, values, and goals.

As a professional athlete, I believed at any given time that I was one of the top players in the league at my position. Regardless of what storm I encountered, I would not change my beliefs about myself as a professional athlete. As a peak performance coach, I believe equally as strongly in my coaching abilities. Of course, I have been coached all my life.

These beliefs provided me with a tremendous amount of confidence in myself and my abilities in those two chosen areas of my life. That was not the case when I first became a real estate professional. I did not have the same beliefs or confidence about myself as a real estate professional.

Although I did not possess the same beliefs in myself in real estate that I had in football or peak performance coaching, I still set high goals for myself as a real estate professional. Understanding the importance of goal setting from my athletic training, I set a goal to close a minimum of 100 transactions a year in real estate by the time I transitioned from football to the game of life. When I look back on things, I am not certain where the number 100 came from. I do recall that it sounded good. I felt if I accomplished my annual real estate goals, I would make a difference in society by helping that number of people meet their needs and achieve their goals.

After you set a goal, you naturally desire to achieve it; you want to hit the target you're aiming for. However, if you don't really believe you can accomplish it, there's a good chance something or someone will knock you off your goal. I was very aware of this and knew that one of the most important steps I needed to take in seeking to accomplish my real estate goals was to assess my beliefs for proper alignment with my vision, mission, and values. I knew that if I was going to utilize my potential in real estate and if I had any chance of attaining my goals, I needed to change my beliefs to be more in alignment with someone who closes 100 transactions per year. That's because your beliefs about yourself can be your most powerful allies or your most potent enemies. What you are able to do in your life depends largely on what you think you can or cannot do.

Once I was conducting a training session with a group of real estate professionals in Phoenix, Arizona, when I paused for a moment to observe the various different gifted and talented people in the group. The individuals taking part in the training came from a wide range of ethnic groups and from a variety of backgrounds. They possessed a broad range of life and business experience.

Those in attendance appeared to have enormous potential. Unfortunately, although blessed with these exceptional gifts and talents, many of them appeared to be using only a small portion of their God-given potential. Why is this?

I believe that it's because of the way we have learned to think about ourselves and the world around us. Many of us have become limited thinkers. We limit ourselves, based on our beliefs.

The way you think, and the way others have learned to think about you, can knock you off your goal, if you do not know how to effectively cope with it. This is why I encourage you to consistently evaluate why you think the way you do and ensure your beliefs are in alignment with your mission, vision, values, and goals in life. While you have great God-given potential, you may not behave in a way that reflects those wonderful gifts. In fact, you may not even realize how much potential you are blessed with.

As I trained the real estate professionals, I could see that some in attendance had a strong difference of opinion with others in the group about how they should approach their business. Some of those with the strongest opinions were not realizing the results they were seeking. Many of their decisions were being driven by the beliefs they held. Although gifted and talented, they were not utilizing their full potential.

The Truth As We See It

We act in accordance with "the truth" as we believe it or perceive it to be. We act accordance with what we think "the truth" is—even if, in reality, we are sadly mistaken.

Says Who?

For example, while growing up you may have been conditioned to believe certain things about yourself: "You're good in sports, but not good in music." "You're good in academics, but not good in sports." Your parents, teachers, coaches, or other authority figures made it clear what they thought about you. You were told over and over again, in words and by the way you were treated, that you were smart or dumb, athletic or clumsy, dependable or lazy, trustworthy or unreliable, valuable and worthy of respect or worthless and deserving of punishment.

You may have grown up without a mother or father in a single-parent household or in an environment where your parents may have been abusive or addicted to alcohol or drugs. Or, you may have grown up in a tough neighborhood, where drugs, alcohol, and violence were a way of life. You may have been treated as if you were inferior. You may still be treated that way today

Through it all, you live and learn. As a child, you have no choice. If you are consistently treated a certain way, after a while, you begin to believe it as "the truth." You begin to think and see that way. And that's where the real damage is done. That's where your God-given potential starts to get blocked. After you begin to see it as "the truth," you begin to act like it, and your performance reflects it.

Choose Your Own Course

The good news is that as a teenager or adult, you can start choosing who you will be and how you will live your life. You can choose your beliefs, thoughts, behaviors and goals, and you can align your beliefs with your vision, mission, and values.

The *Says Who?* approach to life is to search for the truth—the real truth about your God-given potential that allows your light to shine the brightest and not those "truths" that are based on what you have

VISION
(What you really want in life)

MISSION
VALUES

GOALS
NEEDS
OBJECTIVE STEPS

ECONOMIC VEHICLE

BELIEFS

(What you have gotten used to in life)
CURRENT REALITY

been conditioned to believe about yourself, your past failures or experiences, or comments you hear from others who may be operating on limited information or limited thinking.

If you change the way you think, you may well use more of your potential. If you eliminate your mistaken beliefs about yourself and properly align true beliefs about yourself with your vision, mission, and values, you will be better able to remain focused on your goals, even in the midst of a storm.

Chapter 19
Align Beliefs, Habits and Attitudes With Vision

I believe that a career in sales is one of the most dynamic and rewarding professions. Salespeople are some the best paid and most admired people in any business. One of the greatest challenges in sales is avoiding, or recovering from, the dreaded disease of call reluctance. I suffered from this disease early in my real estate career. I was extremely fearful of communicating with a prospective client on the telephone.

With some people, their fears are so great at times when seeking to make a sales call that the handset of a telephone may feel like it weighs 500 pounds to them. For others, they dread making sales calls to such a high degree that they will sometime go to any extreme to avoid making them, even if they are fully aware that this behavior stops them from realizing their vision. Their fears can knock them right off their goals.

For a salesperson, being afraid to make a sales call would be like being afraid of heights for a high-rise window washer. Both professionals will find it very difficult to achieve their goals.

Often people whose lives are driven by fear try desperately to change their behavior. Many have temporary success, but soon they revert back to where they seem to be most comfortable. In an effort to better understand how we can effectively deal with making meaningful and lasting change in this area and others, we will take a closer look at why we think and act the way we do.

Functions of the Mind

Let's first examine the thought process and how our mind works. Our mind works on two levels—the conscious and the subconscious.

The conscious mind has four basic functions: perceive, associate, evaluate, and decide. The thought process works like this:

First, you see or experience something and *perceive* what you think that may be.

Next you *associate* what you see with your past, with what you have seen like this before, in an effort to understand it.

Then you analyze and *evaluate* it, asking yourself: "Is this good or bad for me?" and "What is it leading me toward or away from?"

Finally, you *decide* a course of action, based on the information available to you and the beliefs you hold.

Remember that your assessment, analysis, and decision may be based not on an objective truth, but rather on your subjective beliefs about what is true.

When I entered the real estate profession, I came in with lots of questions about what it actually took to succeed and about my abilities to perform in the business. Many of the decisions I made early on as a real estate professional were based on comments and information from other people in the real estate industry. Much of the information I used at that phase of my growth and development was based on these subjective beliefs, and it showed in my approached to the business. I approached the business with fear and self-doubt, which was not the way I approached my life in sports or peak performance coaching. Although I quickly became aware of this, I experienced some difficulty changing my beliefs in this area. One of the reasons was because of the role of the subconscious mind.

The Subconscious Mind

The subconscious mind is comprised of two parts—the subconscious and the creative subconscious.

The subconscious acts as a recording mechanism. Like a computer memory bank, it records and stores perceptual data and information. Our subconscious has recorded all our past experiences in life. In addition, it has stored what we think, say, and imagine about ourselves, as well as our emotional reactions to those experiences. This adds up to a folder or file of reality we refer to as "the truth."

However, this "truth" may only be seen through the eyes of the beholder; it is not everyone's truth. It may only be the truth as we perceive it or believe it to be. Thus, our picture of reality may be inaccurate or prejudiced if we compare it to an objective interpretation of reality. We may not have recorded the real truth about our individual abilities and potential; rather, we have assumed habits, attitudes, and opinions about ourselves or others we come in contact with.

This became very evident to me early on in my real estate career. We all are different in the world. Each of us is unique in our own way, with different desires and goals in life. In my case, I had a clear vision and mission in life. Achieving my goal of producing 100 transactions per year was a part of that goal. It was one way of my measuring my ability to be the best I could be in the real estate business. Your goals may be different than my goals. That's the beauty of the world we live in.

However, one of the challenges we have in life is what happens when someone who has a goal to produce 100 transactions a year seeks guidance from someone whose goals and aspirations are not in alignment with theirs. That person may provide you with partial, inaccurate or prejudiced information, and if you take it at face value, you may begin to believe it as "the truth." You then record "the truth" on your subconscious in the form of beliefs. Once you deemed it to be true, you begin to carry out those beliefs in the form of your habits and attitudes.

Habits and Attitudes

Our subconscious performs two important functions: control of our habits and control of our attitudes. We will look at what habits and attitudes are and see why they can be so difficult to change. As the world changes around us, it becomes vitally important to discard obsolete habits and attitudes and replace them with useful ones.

Our habits and attitudes are directly related to the subconscious beliefs that we hold about ourselves and the world around us.

Habits. Let's take a look at habits. Our habits are behaviors that have been repeated often enough to be effortless and automatic. They are second-nature patterns we possess. Habits enable us to move smoothly through life. They also allow us to do certain things without thinking about them. Once we learn how or develop the habit pattern, we brush our teeth, tie our shoelaces, go through our normal daily practice and do countless other things as a matter of routine.

Most of our habitual behavior is good for us; it enables us to function efficiently. However, some habits stored on the subconscious level can create obstacles or barriers when we seek to stay focused on our goals or make changes in our lives to become more aligned with our vision, mission, and values. We find ourselves using old habit patterns when trying to deal with new experiences and challenges. These comfortable, yet obsolete, habit patterns can sometimes knock you off your goal.

Our habits stop being good and useful for us at that point when change enters the picture. Once you establish your vision, mission and values, if the objective steps, needs, and goals to realize them dictate that you develop new habit patterns to successfully complete the journey, I encourage you to make a decision to make changes in those areas of your life. Once you've made that decision, I encourage you to take proactive steps to properly align your habits with your vision, mission, and values.

VISION
(What you really want in life)

MISSION
VALUES

GOALS
NEEDS
OBJECTIVE STEPS

ECONOMIC VEHICLE

BELIEFS
HABITS

(What you have gotten used to in life)
CURRENT REALITY

These days, change is becoming more of an everyday occurrence, thanks in part to the world's population becoming more diverse and rapidly developing new technologies. Therefore, the world we live and work in is changing at a rapid pace. The way you used to think and behave may not work in this changing world today.

The same can be said for when you set a goal as part of pursuing your vision. If your goals cause you to venture into new territory, like seeking to transition from one profession to another or increasing your personal income, and you've been trying to make the change without much success, I encourage you to consider what habit patterns you would need to change to bring your habits in alignment with your vision, mission, and values. The habit patterns you have gotten used to in life may not enable you to be most effective and efficient in pursuing your vision.

For many people, changing habits is stressful. Some people seek to avoid, deny, or resist change for as long as possible. But the more they resist, the harder things become for them. Their habits seem to be cast in stone, and they usually blame others for the anxiety and resentment they feel. The good news is that habits can be altered or changed. Taking steps to change your habits to reflect the alignment of your vision, mission, and values will assist you in remaining focused on your goals while in the storm.

Attitudes. Attitudes are similar to habits in that they, too, are sometimes difficult to change. An attitude is a direction in which you lean. It's an emotional response to a perception that you have learned over time. The response can be neutral, positive, or negative. Positive doesn't always mean good, and negative doesn't necessarily mean bad. However, once you set a goal, if you lean toward it, your attitude is thought to be positive; if you lean away from it, your attitude is considered to be negative.

You aren't born with your attitudes—you learn them over time. They start out on the conscious level and through repetition move to the subconscious level.

Your habits and attitudes reflect your subconscious beliefs about who you perceive yourself to be and your expectation of others. When you change those beliefs, your habits and attitudes change easily, effortlessly, and in a natural free-flowing way.

Like your habits, many of your attitudes are good and useful, up to the point when change enters the picture. After establishing your vision, mission, and values, if the steps, needs, and goals to realize your vision require that you change your attitudes in certain areas to successfully complete the journey, I encourage you to commit to making changes in those areas of your life. Once you make that decision, I encourage you to take steps to properly align your attitudes with your vision, mission, and values.

VISION
(What you really want in life)

MISSION
VALUES

GOALS
NEEDS
OBJECTIVE STEPS

ECONOMIC VEHICLE

BELIEFS
HABITS
ATTITUDES

(What you have gotten used to in life)
CURRENT REALITY

The Creative Subconscious

The creative subconscious is the part of our mind that controls our behavior. The difference between the subconscious and creative subconscious is that the subconscious creates the picture that we know ourselves to be, and the creative subconscious acts on that picture.

The creative subconscious has three primary functions:

- First, it causes us to act like the person we know ourselves to be; it maintains our self-image. To maintain sanity, we must act like the subconscious picture we hold of ourselves.
- Second, the creative subconscious creatively solves problems. The problems are solved in a natural, free-flowing manner.
- Third, the creative subconscious provides energy and drive. When it senses a problem or obstacle standing in the way of our goal, the creative subconscious provides great drive, energy, and motivation to find answers and a solution.

So, if you are a salesperson who dislikes receiving phone calls at home or if you fear being rejected by the person you're calling, the first time you think the person you've called replies in a rude manner, your creative subconscious will go to work to solve the problem. One function of the creative subconscious is to solve the conflict that occurs when the image you have of yourself does not match events in your external environment. This conflict is not all bad; in some cases, the conflict may be constructive. In fact, creating this kind of challenge for yourself is a good thing. The clearer your vision and goals become to you, the more discontent you will find with your current reality. And your creative subconscious will go to work searching for ways to resolve the conflict.

At the same time, you are adjusting your subconscious beliefs about who you know yourself to be and what you can do. You are creating tremendous drive and energy to achieve your goals and make the changes in your life you desire. This energy can greatly assist you in making necessary changes to enable you to remain focused on your goals, even when you are caught in a storm.

Chapter 20
Align Expectations With Vision

If you dislike receiving sales calls at home, or if you have a fear of rejection, you can probably think back in your life to an event that contributed to the beliefs you hold today in those areas.

If you once fell short or failed at a task and were told that you would never succeed at that thing, you might translate that comment into a belief that you "lack what it takes" to succeed. As we talked about earlier, this becomes "the truth" in your eyes, based on the lens you are looking through. Based on the truth as you believe it or perceive it to be, you go about living your life based on those beliefs.

When you explore where many of the beliefs you hold today came from, you may discover that much of the knowledge you use to determine "the truth" in your life comes from generalizations you draw from your experience and conditioning. For example, based on your experience with receiving or making sales calls, if you believe that calling someone at home or work is an invasion of their privacy, you may conclude that all people do not want to be interrupted at home or work by a sales call. So, an important question to ask yourself is, "Where do the beliefs I hold come from?"

This is an important question to ask and answer, because some generalizations you make in life are based on limited experience, misinformation, or your perception of "the truth." For example, if

one of the first 25 people you come into contact with while making sales calls reacts in what you perceive to be a rude manner, you may be willing to conclude that most or all people feel that it's an invasion of their privacy to receive sales calls at home. This belief can knock you off your goal.

Based on the tenacity and power of your beliefs, you may search for information to validate what you perceive to be the truth. You become selective in searching for information that will reinforce your beliefs. This persistence is evident when we have conflicting beliefs or attitudes, such as "I know I need to make the sales calls in order to achieve my sales goals; however, I have a strong fear of rejection if I make that sales call."

When you experience such a conflict, you tend to be biased in your search for information to validate your strongest beliefs. In your search for information to support your beliefs, your approach might become so biased that it leads to a distorted view of the facts. You might become so persistent in your pursuit of what you believe to be the truth, that you lose track of your goal.

The Self-fulfilling Prophecy

Another factor that increases the persistence with which you pursue what you deem to be the truth is the self-fulfilling prophecy: You may act on your beliefs in such a way that you bring about the expected results you are seeking. For example, salespeople who think that the person on the other end of the call may be rude to them may act in a manner that causes them to be hesitant in speaking to the person during the call, even though the person on the other end of the line may be cordial and polite. These salespeople are acting in a manner consistent with their expectations.

Expectations influence our behavior in such a way as to validate them. We often are willing to allow certain experiences in our life to override substantial amounts of statistical information. For example, the salesperson may read about a survey of 1,000 sales calls, indicating that people do not feel their privacy is being violated if they receive a call, only to disregard the information when a friend says, "I received a call from a salesperson that interrupted our dinner, and I did not like it."

When you hold certain beliefs, which may not be in alignment with your vision, mission, and values, negative comments can knock you off your goal. Therefore I encourage you to take steps to properly align your "expectations" with your vision, mission, and values.

VISION
(What you really want in life)

MISSION
VALUES

GOALS
NEEDS
OBJECTIVE STEPS

ECONOMIC VEHICLE

BELIEFS
HABITS
ATTITUDES
EXPECTATIONS

(What you have gotten used to in life)

CURRENT REALITY

Expectations play a vital role in all our lives. Aligning expectations with vision, mission, and values seems to be a difficult task for some people because of how they have learned to think and what they have put into their subconscious.

Says Who?

Again, the subconscious part of our mind is where our beliefs are stored. It is a storehouse for those things that we have decided are true in our lives.

Often those beliefs have much more to do with other people's opinions than with the real truth. Remember the conditioning process that you have gone through to develop the beliefs, habits, and attitudes you hold today. Be aware that many of your opinions about yourself and others may be based on limited information or limited thinking, making them biased beliefs.

If you hold obsolete or mistaken beliefs based on the way you have been conditioned to think, you will behave as if they were true. If the comments you hear from others are based on obsolete or mistaken beliefs or the way they have been conditioned to think and you take them out of context or for face value, you behave as if they were true. Remember: You act not in accordance with the truth, but the truth as you believe it or perceive it to be.

Your beliefs possess enormous power. Basically, your thoughts about what is true through your eyes help guide your behavior. Based on how your subconscious works, any behavior that you seek, which conflicts with your beliefs tends to quickly disappear. The part of your mind that helps achieve this function is your creative subconscious, which assures that you act the way you know yourself to be.

When you behave in ways that do not reflect the person you know yourself to be, your creative subconscious goes to work to correct the picture. It corrects the "mistake" by changing your behavior back to fit your self-image—the dominant picture you have of yourself. Even if you are trying to change for the better, if your subconscious believes that "better" is not like you, it will automatically ensure that your efforts to change fail. That's why it's important to begin the process of change first on the inside with the subconscious, by first changing your beliefs.

That's also why "trying harder" doesn't always work. If your deepest beliefs about yourself are that you can't succeed or you don't deserve to succeed, you won't succeed, no matter how hard you try. Based on those beliefs, your creative subconscious will find a way to make sure you fail in your efforts to succeed. Once you change your dominant internal picture of yourself to that of a successful person, your efforts to make a change for the better will begin to pay off. In effect, you are creating change beyond pretense.

Again, lasting change starts on the inside. If you are trying to make the changes you deem necessary to achieve your goals, I encourage you to first change the way you think in certain areas. Properly align your expectations with your vision, mission, and values. Behind everything you do is a thought. Every behavior is motivated by a belief, and every action is prompted by an attitude. If you desire to stay focused on your goals and change your life for the better, I encourage you to start first on the inside by aligning your thoughts and beliefs with what you really want in life.

Realizing your goals and becoming the person you desire to become begins with a decision to grow personally. Can you imagine world-class athletes desiring to be the best in the world in their fields and deciding that they are not going to work on developing the skills but simply show up on game day and perform? No, not at all!

Elite professional athletes wake up each day and ask themselves, "How can I be better today than yesterday and how can I be better tomorrow than I am today?" This requires on-going personal and professional growth and development, as well as consistent skill development to be the best they can be. The same process will enable

you to remain focused on your goals despite your circumstances, things not going as planned, or comments you hear from others.

Chapter 21
Narrow Focus, Big Picture

What do Barry Bonds, Hank Aaron, and Babe Ruth have in common? Each of them is considered to be one of the greatest home run hitters in major league baseball history. They have something else in common. In order to improve their effectiveness as a hitter, each of them, like many other great hitters in baseball, narrow their focus while at bat, with a goal of increasing their efficiency (batting average and slugging average).

Each of these men was blessed with exceptional gifts and talents. To assure that they utilize more of their God-given potential as a hitter while at bat, they would select a portion of home plate that they considered to be their hitting zone. They would lock-out the area of weakness and lock-on to the hitting zone portion of the plate. When a pitch was made in this designated area, they would not only make contact with the pitch, often they would hit a home run.

When opponents became aware of their hitting zone, pitchers would try to avoid giving them a good pitch to hit. But these feared home run hitters often remained patient at the plate, locked-on to their hitting zone, waiting for their pitch to hit.

With less than two strikes on them, rarely would they swing at any pitch outside their designated hitting zone. With two strikes on them, they would protect the plate but still look for a pitch in their hitting zone. When they saw their pitch, because they had locked-on to what they wanted to accomplish and locked-out other options, they were better able to utilize more of their God-given potential.

What can we all learn from the great home run hitters? Well, their ability to select and focus on a hitting zone, without losing sight of the big picture, enabled them to increase their focus and utilize more of their God-given gifts and talents.

What might prevent you and me from utilizing a similar approach in our lives? One is a lack of focus in the right areas of your life. We each have a wide range of areas we can focus on in life: our work, our health, our marriage, our children, our problems, the economy, the national debt. Over some areas, we have either direct or indirect control. But over other areas, we have little or no control. Highly effective people and high-performance individuals invest their time, effort, and energy on things over which they have direct or indirect control, and they lock-out those things over which they have no control. Like the great home run hitters, they select an area that they focus on.

Highly effective people separate those things over which they have no particular control by creating a circle of focus. Inside the circle, they place those things they have either direct or indirect control over. This is a technique used very effectively by high-performance individuals and elite athletes.

Jack Youngblood, one of the all-time great Rams players, had a favorite saying: "Don't worry about the mule, just load the wagon." This favorite saying was his way of telling his teammates—especially the young ones—to keep their focus on taking care of their business first, and the rest of the team members would take care of their own.

Taking care of your business first requires you to have faith and confidence in yourself, as well as in your family members or teammates. What Jack was telling us is that the mule will take care of his job of pulling the wagon, as long as we take care of our job of loading it. He was trying to tell us that we did not need to concern ourselves about anything other than loading the wagon properly; the pulling of the wagon was out of our control. All we needed to do was take care of our business.

In your life, there are things over which you have no control and others areas you can do something about. Highly effective people focus on areas where they have direct or indirect control inside their circle of focus, and place those things over which they have no control outside the circle in their area of no control.

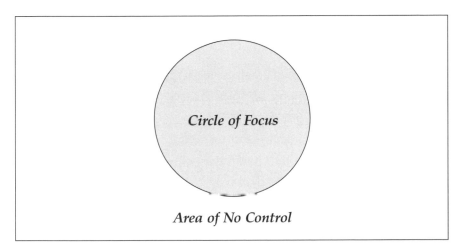

Circle of Focus

Area of No Control

By determining which of these two areas we are to focus most of our time and energy, we can better position ourselves to be more effective, utilize more of our potential, and remain focused on our goals. Just as the great home run hitters focus on a specific zone, highly effective people focus their efforts inside their circle of focus. When they find themselves in a storm, they proactively work on those things they can do something about.

Conversely, those individuals who waste their time and energy on things over which they have no control often find themselves emotionally reacting to the storms in their lives. They focus on the weaknesses of other people or circumstances over which they have no control. Their focus results in blaming and accusing others for the storms in their lives. The negative energy generated by their misplaced focus of their time and energy, combined with neglect in the areas they can do something about, causes them to lose focus of their goals.

In narrowing your focus, without losing site of the big picture, the problems you face usually fall in one of three areas: *direct control*, problems involving your own behavior; *indirect control*, problems involving other people's behavior; or *no control*, things you can do nothing about, such as your past.

Working on your beliefs, habits, attitudes, and expectations can assist you in solving many of your direct control problems. These problems fall within your circle of focus.

You can effectively address indirect control problems that involve other people's behavior by changing the way you deal with them. Most people try reasoning to deal with these problems. If that doesn't work, they may fight or escape the problem by running away.

Although, you can't control the behavior of others in your life, you can control your reaction to their behavior; hence, indirect control problems are placed inside the circle of focus.

Dealing with no-control problems involves learning to genuinely accept them, whether we like them or not. Although we can't control these problems, we can control how we react to them. If it's something you can't do anything about, I encourage you to "let it go." With this approach, you do not empower these problems to control you. They are clearly outside your circle of focus and in your area of no control.

Highly effective people make a habit of not empowering those things in their lives that they have no control over. For example, professional athletes often play in hostile environments or bad weather conditions and yet remain focused on their goals, despite playing when the weather is 10 degrees below zero, with a wind-chill factor of -20 degrees, and frozen ground. The players sometimes find themselves 3,000 miles from home, playing in front of 70,000 hostile fans who are all cheering against them. The players are requested to perform in what some may consider the worst possible environments for utilizing more of their God-given potential.

As a fan, you turn on your TV in the comfort of your living room, and yet you not only expect your favorite team to play well in a hostile environment, you expect them to perform at their best and win. If you have watched elite athletes perform at the highest level when the weather conditions reflected sunny and 72 degrees, you do not lower your expectations of their performance merely because they have to perform in a storm.

Personally, I have found myself in that hostile environment on a number of occasions as a professional athlete. My coaches would often ask: "Can we do anything about the weather or the conditions?" And "Will your opponents have to play in the same conditions?" If the answer to the first question is "no" and the answer to the second question is "yes," then the best thing to do is not to worry about it, because you can't control the situation anyway. If you can't control the situation, focus only on those things you can control directly—such as the execution of your game plan.

When you evaluate the performances of world-class athletes in storms, you recognize one key to their success is their ability to focus their time, efforts and energies on things they can control. One of the primary reasons why they are able to remain focused is their ability to "separate emotion from logic" while in the storm.

Says Who?

Emotions drive many of the decisions we make in life. If we feel uncomfortable in a particular situation, we tend to shy away from the situation or retreat back to an area where we feel more comfortable. The situation brings about certain emotions in the form of stress and anxiety within us. Those emotions can cause us to make decisions that may not be in alignment with our vision, mission, and values.

Another area where our emotions can cause us a challenge is when we are confronted with a situation where something we believe to be right in our eyes is violated. When our beliefs and the situation we find ourselves in don't match, we experience a certain set of emotions. Depending on what drives us, we can become overwhelmed with the situation or with someone else as a result of the emotions.

For example, you can become so overwhelmed with frustration and anger that these emotions lead you to making decisions that are not in alignment with your vision, mission, and values. These wrong reactions and behaviors can knock you off your goal.

Each day you encounter many different situations that can lead to storms. When you find yourself in the storm, keep in mind that it may not be the circumstance that is causing the problem; it may be some of your subconscious beliefs. Where you place your focus while in the storm may be causing the problem. Tough circumstances just bring those beliefs to the surface.

For example, if you know yourself to be an impatient person, you may find that the longer you are stuck in traffic, the more your stress level increases. As your anxiety increases, you may completely lose sight of your goal of arriving safely at your intended destination. A simple honk of a horn from someone seeking to merge into your traffic lane may be enough to stir such hot emotions that you express your frustrations in an angry or violent manner. This reaction could have more to do with your subconscious beliefs and where you are placing your focus than the actual circumstances.

Usually, your emotions operate at their peak during storms. The better you manage your emotions when hit with storms in your life, the better you'll remain focused on your goals.

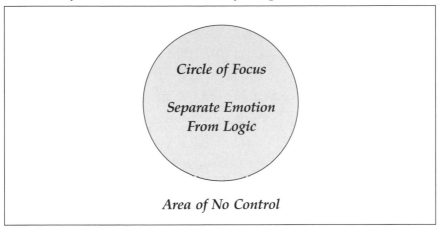

Circle of Focus

Separate Emotion From Logic

Area of No Control

Highly effective people have a unique way of separating emotion from logic when dealing with those things that fall within their "Circle of Focus."

I encourage you to take the approach used by world-class athletes and other highly effective people and not allow anyone or anything to have so much control over you that it affects the way you live your life or conduct your business. If you have control of something, lock-on to it; if you do not have control of it, lock it out. Focus your time and energies only on things that you control. By concentrating your attention in this area, you greatly improve your ability to remain focused on your goal.

Consider a basketball player who must shoot free throws into the faces of a hostile crowd that is waving signs, banners, balloons (and just about anything else they can get their hands on) behind the

basket. The next time you watch a basketball game, notice how the elite players handle the distractions. The player focuses only on the rim of the basket—on what he or she can control.

If you do not have control over something, I encourage you not to worry about it. Don't let it affect you. When dealing with no control problem areas, what you lock-on to and lock-out is key, along with how quickly you adapt to the unfamiliar surroundings. Basketball players have control over shooting free throws, so they lock-on to the front of the rim of the basket and lock-out potential distractions, such as the fans behind the basket, because they have no control over them. They are outside their "circle of focus." They lock-on to their game plan, over which they have control; they lock-out the booing and the hostile crowd, over which they have no control. That is where world-class athletes place their focus in a hostile environment or bad weather. They only concern themselves with the things they can do something about.

Whether a problem is *direct*, *indirect* or *no control*, you can seek a solution based on where you choose to focus your time, efforts, and energy. In choosing your response to the storms in your life, you positively and proactively affect the situation you find yourself in. Once you determine what's inside your "circle of focus," take responsibility for your reaction to the storms in your life. Where you focus your time, effort, and energy is a vital part of that process.

Highly effective people change from the inside out by seeking first to change those things they control. This enables them to remain focused on their goals, even when they are caught in a storm.

The *Says Who?* approach is to be personally accountable for your own behavior and focus on improving your skill set. With this approach, you will better position yourself to take proactive steps in closing the gap between current reality and vision.

Section 6
Keep on Course

At the very heart of our *circle of focus* is our ability to make and keep commitments and promises that are in alignment with our vision, mission, and values. The commitments and promises we make to ourselves and to others are within our *circle of focus,* and they are at the apex of the *Says Who?* approach in a proactive way. They should lead us toward attainment of our goals. They are also at the center of our personal growth and development and our skill development.

Chapter 22
Keep Personal Commitments and Promises

As we make and keep commitments and promises, even small ones, we gain the self-control, courage, and strength to accept more responsibility for our own lives. By making and keeping promises to ourselves and others, we enhance our reputation with ourselves by doing what we say we're going to do. We become more authentic.

As we recognize areas we desire to change or grow, and act on them, we take proactive steps to close the gap between current reality and our vision. We grow personally and professionally, and we build character, as we set goals and make and keep promises—and remain true to them. Making and keeping commitments and promises makes possible every positive thing in our lives, even in storms.

Focus on Goals

Here we can find two ways to assist us in remaining focused on our goals during storms. We can make a commitment or promise and keep it, or we can set a goal and work to achieve it, even in storms. With a clear purpose and vision in life, and a solid set of values, making and keeping commitments and promises will assist you in growing, both personally and professionally, and in aligning your beliefs, habits, attitudes, and expectations with your vision, mission, and values.

Says Who?

Making commitments and promises and keeping them daily will assist you in dealing with the storms you encounter in life and with the normal events of each day. By dealing with the normal events of daily life, you develop the proactive ability to handle the unexpected pressures of the storms when you encounter them. So, assess daily how well you make and keep commitments. Take small steps each day to keep your commitments.

For example, if you set a goal to be more patient, I encourage you to make small commitments and keep them to attain your goal. You can be part of the solution, not part of the problem. You can focus on other people's strengths, not on their weaknesses. When things are not going as planned, you don't demean, belittle, or degrade yourself or others. When you make a mistake, you don't blame others; instead, you admit it, accept it, correct it, learn from it, and let it go. In tough situations, you work on things you have control over. You work on you! You work on being authentic.

By being true to yourself, by making and keeping commitments and promises to yourself, you start living your life by design. You start living the life you desire. Should you not keep your commitments and promises in life, you live life by default. You empower other people and circumstances outside of your *circle of focus* to shape much of your life by default. You hold many of the beliefs, habits, attitudes, and expectations you hold today because of your past conditioning.

Make and Keep Promises

Should you ever desire to make a positive change in your life, I encourage you to make and keep commitments and promises. Should you fail to take this step, you will continue to reactively live the scripts handed to you by your past conditioning and other people's pressures and circumstances.

During the coaching process at World Class Coaches, we have discovered that many people seek to be all things to all people. Their inability to "say no" leads them to operate on a variety of fronts at the same time. Many of the commitments and promises they make dissipate under the pressures of trying to be all things to all people.

Many people find this inability to make and keep promises to be a major challenge for them. It contributes to them living a life of chaos, with no end in sight. If you find yourself in this predicament, you may want to ask yourself, "What precisely am I seeking to accomplish in my life, and why?" Once you determine what that is, I encourage you to commit to making changes in those areas that may not be in alignment with your vision, mission, and values. Once you make the commitment, I encourage you to keep it. This process will assist you in remaining focused on your goals while in the storm.

Chapter 23
Control Your Self-Talk

Who you perceive yourself to be plays a large role in how you think and behave.

So, I invite you to take a close look at your thought patterns, and the role they play in creating and maintaining your self-image through the way you talk to yourself. These inner, usually silent ,conversations are called *self-talk*. We often refer to them as "those little voices" talking to us in our head.

More often than not, they take the form of thoughts—thoughts about you, your activities, feelings, and experiences. These thoughts trigger pictures that cause feelings or emotions.

Take Self-Talk Seriously

On the surface, self-talk may seem like just innocent words, pictures, and feelings; but self-talk is taken seriously by your subconscious. In fact, your self-talk helps shape and form your self-image. So, don't underestimate the importance of your self-talk.

Don't believe the old saying, "Sticks and stones may break my bones, but words can never hurt me." Words can do as much damage to your self-image as sticks and stones can do to your body. When other people try to tear you down with what they say to you, it can be painful and destructive. However, their words cannot hurt you unless you take them for face value and accept them as the truth. It's what you tell yourself about their words that does the damage. If you reject their negative comments and substitute your own positive truths, their words will not affect you.

Over time, people who are in the habit of belittling themselves and putting themselves down through negative self-talk develop a negative self-image. People who are in the habit of commending and encouraging themselves through positive self-talk develop a positive self-image.

Self-Talk Impacts Self-Image

As a professional athlete, I saw myself as being one of the best at my position in the National Football League. That was the image I had of myself as a player. I utilized positive self-talk daily to affirm and enhance those beliefs in me.

As a real estate professional, I saw myself as an athlete in a business suit when I first entered the business. I often affirmed that image through my self-talk by affirming the very things I was seeking to avoid. I knew that if I truly desired to achieve my real estate goals, I must first change my beliefs about myself as a real estate professional. In order to successfully accomplish this goal, I knew I must change my self-talk to be in alignment with my real estate goals. That's because of how self-talk impacts self-image.

Your self-talk plays a vital role in establishing and maintaining your self-image, which is a culmination of the all the beliefs you hold about yourself. Your beliefs influence your daily behavior. And your behavior, more than anything else, determines the results you get and the success you can expect to experience in life. Your self-talk can lead you to happiness and success. But, it can also knock you off of your goal.

Imagine a balance scale inside your mind—an attitudinal balance scale that weighs your attitude about yourself. One side is positive,

and the other is negative. Every time you devalue yourself, belittle yourself, call yourself names, ridicule yourself, or put yourself down, you add a little weight to the negative side of the scale. Every time you praise, congratulate, commend, encourage, compliment, affirm or build yourself up, you add weight to the positive side.

So, every bit of your self-talk carries weight. The scale goes up and down, depending on whether you build yourself up or tear yourself down. The balance of the scale will shift toward the negative or the positive, to one side or the other, depending on the nature of your self-talk. As your self-talk shifts, so too does your self-image.

Negative self-talk reflects a negative self-image.

Positive self-talk reflects a positive self-image.

Says Who?

Other-Talk Can Impact Self-Talk

What happens when other people put you down or build you up with what they say to you? Does their talk have the same impact as what you say to yourself? Yes, if you buy into it and accept it as the truth. But if you reject what another person has to say about you, their opinion won't have an impact on you. However, you have to really reject it, not simply pretend to reject it, knowing the impact it can have on you and your self-image

If what they say is negative, I encourage you to counter it with a positive truth of your own. You don't have to do it out loud, but you need to counteract it. The good news is that no one can tear you down, but you. But that's also the bad news if you have the habit of tearing yourself down.

The Johnson Way

When our oldest son was very young, he was extremely shy. When he met or greeted people, he would stare at the ground or display other shy mannerisms. As he became older and came into contact with more people, many of them would reaffirm his shy tendencies by saying things like, "You are so shy." Hearing these comments over and over from others, along with the thought patterns he was developing in his mind as part of his normal self-talk, confirmed his shyness each time he met someone or when someone reminded him that his behavior shows he is shy.

My wife Julie and I became very concerned about our son's shy behavior and wondered how it would affect his self-image as he grew older. As we watched him, his discomfort became more obvious, as he came into contact with more people. So, we decided to institute the *Johnson Way to Greet People*. I learned this technique from former University of Texas coach, Darrel Royal.

This technique calls for each family member to greet people by looking them right in the eyes and extending a firm handshake when appropriate. We explained that when you look someone in the eyes when you are talking to them, you show respect for the person you are greeting, as well as respect for yourself. We explained to them that you also display self-confidence when you look someone in the eyes when you're talking to them.

We talked about what it means to have respect for others and for ourselves. When our three kids started using this technique, my wife and I would ask them, "What does it mean to look someone in the eyes when you greet them?" The answer we received from them was "Confidence."

If our kids greeted someone without using the *Johnson Way*, we simply said to them, "Where are you supposed to look when you greet someone?" They responded "in the eyes." We then ask them, "What does that mean?" And the response we get is, "It means confidence." This technique positively counteracts the negative comments my son was hearing from others, and thereby impacts his self-talk and self-esteem.

Successful people are in the habit of seeing the best in themselves and affirming it with their thoughts and words. They're not bragging; they are building themselves up by confirming their own ability and potential. Being modest is a good thing, up to a point. The more you affirm and confirm your strengths, the stronger you'll be. The more you affirm your ability to learn and grow, the more learning and growing you will do. The more learning and growing you do, the better you remain focused on your goals. Changing my self-talk played a vital role in changing my beliefs to be more in alignment with my goals in real estate.

Chapter 24
Affirm the Desired Outcome You Seek

One of my goals as a real estate professional was to align my activities and behavior in real estate with the success patterns I was accustomed to in sports. In addition to controlling my self-talk, another step I took to build my self-image as a real estate professional was to affirm my goals daily. As an athlete, I used these techniques religiously.

Beyond controlling your self-talk, another step you can take to build your self-image is to affirm your goals daily. Affirmation helps you to make changes in the areas you desire from the inside out.

When you seek to align your behavior with your vision, mission, and values, if you try to change from the outside in, you may struggle to maintain the new behavior, because of the unnatural feelings you experience. However, if you work from the inside out, you will experience lasting change, greater use of your natural potential, and better focus on your goals.

Daily, you affirm things in your mind: "I am not a disciplined person." "I am not good at that." "I am not a good cook." "I am not a patient person." "I am an early riser." "I have a hot temper." "I like to shop." These affirmations can impact your life, if you accept them as the truth.

An affirmation is simply a statement of truth—your truth. Affirmations are not magical, but they are potent. The technique of using affirmations and visualization is taught to world-class athletes and used by other highly effective people and high-performance individuals—from airline pilots to entertainers and salespeople.

Subconscious Scripting

One reason why affirmations have such an impact on our belief system is because our subconscious can't tell the difference between something vividly imagined and a real experience. That's why dreams feel so real to us. That's also why so many professional athletes, health care professionals, salespeople, and other highly effective people and high-performance individuals use these techniques.

Affirmations are powerful statements that can deeply affect your subconscious mind. Because your subconscious accepts anything you vividly imagine as reality, visualizing and affirming your goals empowers you to attain them. You can develop the habit of affirming the changes you're seeking and visualizing yourself in the new behavior you desire. This process will eliminate much of the stress and pushback that accompanies change efforts. It's a very effective way to create change from the inside out.

Affirming the changes you are seeking daily simply means you control what you are affirming. You affirm the changes you are seeking to align your behavior with your vision, mission, and values. For example, if you are seeking to lose weight and become a healthier and more energetic person, you may write an affirmation that reads, "I am a healthy and vibrant person."

Because of the potential impact of affirmations, for better or for worse, I encourage you to learn how to write affirmations correctly. This will assist you in creating powerful visual images that bring about the right pictures and emotions when you are reading your affirmation. This will also assist you in simulating the desired outcome you are pursuing.

Flight Simulation

For example, suppose you are on an airplane flight, and in mid-flight one of the engines fails. How long would you want the pilot to think about what needs to be done? You want him or her to react automatically. You want a sure-handed and lightning-fast response. And you'll probably get it, because that pilot spent many hours in a flight simulator preparing for just such a situation.

When you practice using affirmations and visualization regularly, you are stepping inside your own simulator. You are experiencing—through vivid, detailed mental pictures—exactly what you want to happen to you and how you desire to behave. You are simulating the experience you desire.

Guidelines for Writing

To better assist you in writing your affirmations correctly, I encourage you to utilize the following guidelines:

1. Affirmations are personal. Make your affirmations "I" statements; they must be about you. You can't affirm change in anyone else's behavior, and no one else can make change happen for you. See yourself doing and feeling whatever it is you affirm, and describe it.

2. Affirmations are phrased positively. Affirmations describe what you want to be and do, not what you don't want or are trying to avoid. Don't say, "I no longer lose my temper when I feel angry." Say "I remain calm and reasonable, even when angry."

3. Affirmations take place in the present. Picture your goal as already accomplished. See what it will be like when the problem is solved. You want to imagine and describe a new current reality, not future possibilities. You already have the ability to do what you need to do—you don't need to affirm that. Affirm the use of the ability. See it as if it is happening right now and describe it in the present tense.

4. Affirmations describe achievement. Affirm the success, not the effort. Affirm action and accomplishment, and see it in detail, including sights, sounds, smells, tastes and everything else you can think of to make your picture come to life in your mind.

5. Affirmations make no comparisons. Don't compete with anyone or compare yourself to anyone else. You and your talents and skills are unique. Compete against yourself to be better today than yesterday, and better tomorrow than you are today.

6. Affirmations describe action. See yourself in action, doing exactly as you want to be able to do it. Describe the action as precisely as possible.

7. Affirmations are emotional. Simple repetition of an affirmation won't have much effect. You must feel your affirmations and have an emotional response to them. How will you feel when your goal is achieved? Describe the feeling, and allow yourself to actually experience the feeling. Goals that have powerful emotional payoffs are far more likely to be met than those you think you are "supposed to," or "have to" meet.

8. Affirmations are accurate. Don't allow your affirmations to become far-fetched fantasies. If you don't really believe you have the ability to make it happen, how can you affirm it in a believable way? See yourself achieving your goals in the real world.

9. Affirmations balance your life. Affirm success for yourself in all the key areas of your life. Don't limit your affirmations to your business. Seek a life that is well balanced, one with positive change in all the key areas of your life.

10. Affirmations are realistic. Affirm achievements that will make you stretch your capabilities, but don't go overboard. Don't seek to affirm perfection and avoid words like *always* or *never*. Set challenging goals, but not beyond what you think you can accomplish with focused effort. If you set your goals too far out, you'll lose drive and energy. Only you know what is realistic for you, but don't sell yourself short. Be realistic while staying optimistic.

11. Affirmations should be shared carefully. Be careful when sharing your goals and affirmations. Tell only those people who support you and believe in your ability to grow and achieve your goals. You neither want nor need negative feedback from people who may not want to see you grow. Tell only those people who are willing and able to help you.

12. Affirmations are repeated daily. As athletes, we read our scouting report, game plan and affirm our goals daily. With consistent repetition, we seek to consciously repeat the desired outcome we were seeking so often that it became a subconscious habit pattern. Once there, it would become a part of us, where we perform the task naturally and effortless. I encourage you to read your affirmation statements daily, even several times a day. As you read them, think about what a healthy and vibrant person may look like, if that's an area you're seeking to make a change in. Visualize yourself looking, acting, and feeling like the healthy vibrant person you desire to be. I encourage you to repeat this process several times. Read it when you wake up in the morning and just before you go to bed each night. Repeat the process several times during the day. Repetition is vital. The more you repeat the affirmation with the right spirit of intent, the greater impact it will have on your subconscious.

The more I was able to use the tools as a real estate professional that I was accustomed to using as a professional athlete, the more aligned my behavior became with my goals and vision in real estate. The more I controlled my self-talk and affirmed my goals daily, the more my self-image changed from that of a pro football player in a

business suit to that of a real estate professional who played pro football. This change helped bring about a dramatic change in the results I began to experience in the real estate industry, as I moved closer to realizing my real estate goals.

When your affirmations are written correctly and when you make this process a part of your daily routine, you'll find yourself using much more of your potential. You'll see yourself growing and changing in positive ways because affirmations give you a vivid mental experience of success. When you create this successful experience over and over again, it becomes assimilated into your self-image. It becomes "like you" to behave that way. And, affirmations will assist you in remaining focused on your goals.

Chapter 25
Internalize Your Vision

You became the person you are today in current reality largely due to your conditioning. You've gotten used to certain habits and attitudes, certain ideas about how you perceive yourself and those around you, and certain ways of doing things. Now you don't even think about them. They have been engrained into your subconscious.

Although some of the patterns you possess today may not be aligned with your vision, mission, and values, you're familiar and comfortable with them.

If you desire to make changes to become more productive and focused on your goals, I encourage you to start with a decision to change and develop a clear picture of what you want. However, a decision and a statement of affirmation and visualization are not enough.

Imprint and Assimilate

I was well aware that I became the professional athlete I became because of the conditioning I had experienced. The picture I had of myself as a football player was very strong and vivid, squarely in my subconscious, because of my conditioning.

It was my desire to duplicate that process as a real estate professional. I continued to take those steps, and my confidence level began to soar as I gained more opportunities to demonstrate my skills as a real estate professional. I can attribute that increase in con-

fidence in part to my internalizing my vision as a real estate professional and seeing myself as one of world's best real estate professionals. Feeling focused, confident and faithful, I was fortunate enough to achieve my real estate goals by closing more than 100 transactions a year and acquiring the valuable business experience recommended by my mentor, Lou Tice.

If you desire to make meaningful change in your life, I encourage you to imprint the new picture of your vision into your subconscious. In other words, make your vision stronger and more dominant than current reality.

Again, I encourage you to *imprint* the new picture of your vision into your subconscious. In other words, *I encourage you to make your vision stronger and more dominant than current reality.*

Through *assimilation,* you bring your goal fully into your life. You make the picture of what you want stronger and more dominant than your current reality; stronger and more vivid than what you are used to in life.

When you assimilate something, it becomes second nature to you; it becomes natural and free-flowing. It becomes like you; it fits your picture of who you are. The process of assimilation is what makes the pursuit of your goals an exciting adventure instead of an anxiety trip.

Mentors, Models, Coaches

Good role models, mentors, and coaches can play a major role in assisting you in internalizing your vision. Remember, your self-image plays a role in determining the goals you set for yourself; what you are ready, willing, and able to do; and how much of your God-given potential you will utilize to achieve them.

Good mentors and coaches can assist you in building a strong, confident, and resilient self-image. They can help you reinforce your beliefs in your ability to change for the better and utilize more of your potential. Good mentors and coaches usually see more in you than you see in yourself, so they can help you remain focused on your goals. They remind you to "keep your eye on the ball."

When the ball—your new vision or goal—becomes your dominant picture, you will be more motivated to make it happen and to change current reality to match your picture. That's because your creative subconscious generates drive, energy, and ideas to assist you in realizing your goals. Any obstacles or barriers you may encounter will just make you more determined to overcome them.

Goal-setting is making a decision about what you want to get used to. It might be driving a new car or working at a more satisfying job. It could be good health and physical fitness, or a happy, harmonious marriage. Maybe it's building a successful business or doubling your income. Whatever it is, you have the potential and the ability to achieve it.

What's Next?

What happens after you achieve your goals and move current reality into your vision?

Once you achieve your goal, the creative subconscious no longer has a conflict to resolve, because there is no longer a gap between vision and current reality. So, it turns off the energy and drive. When this takes place, what happens to your motivation? It goes flat, unless you create another gap by setting another goal to achieve.

So, goal-setting is an ongoing process. The trick is to keep achieving and then setting new, higher goals. That way, your drive and energy keeps flowing.

You get used to the new and become dissatisfied with the old. Then, you create a better vision, a better goal, and make it part of your life. You affirm it, visualize it, and make the picture of the new stronger than current reality. You use the power of your creative subconscious to keep your motivation strong. During the process, you unleash more of your potential, and life just keeps getting better and better.

Applied Affirmations

Affirmations, correctly written and applied, have immense power to help you achieve your goals. Written affirmations provide a framework for visualization and a blueprint for remaining focused on your goals. They are goal statements that help you move forward with minimal stress and anxiety into the life you desire. With them, you position yourself to anticipate and effectively handle change in a natural, free-flowing way.

Now that you know how to write affirmations correctly, you're ready to learn how to put them to work for you. You're ready to learn the powerful process by which you internalize these pictures of goal achievements into your subconscious.

My mentor, Lou Tice, taught me a valuable formula: I x V = R. This formula is something you have been using all your life.

Imagination. The "I" stands for imagination. As a kid, you had a very vivid imagination. For example, when you were looking forward to Christmas or your birthday, you were imagining what it would look like on Christmas day or your birthday, as you looked forward to opening gifts. Now, when you plan a sales presentation, you imagine what it will look like and how you would desire it to go.

Vividness. The "V" stands for vividness. The more vivid the pictures in your mind are, the more real they will be to your subconscious. If I ask you to picture any animal, who really knows what it would look like? But if I request that you imagine a three-year-old black stallion, standing in his stall, wearing a brown saddle with a red and white bridal, you have a much more vivid picture. So, strive for specific detail.

Reality. The "R" represents reality. If you imagine something vividly and add emotion to the picture, your subconscious will accept it as reality. Clarity, vivid detail, and emotions are keys to internalizing your affirmations successfully. This plants your affirmations in the soil of your subconscious mind. When you can actually experience, in your mind, what you are saying and picturing, your subconscious will record it as a real event. When you do it repeatedly over time, you gradually change your self-image. Your affirmed behavior becomes a natural, free-flowing part of who you are.

Mind Over Time

It doesn't take long to repeat and visualize an affirmation, but it does take focus and concentration. If you simply say the words without vividly picturing or feeling them, you'll find that little or nothing will change. As you repeat your affirmations, put your heart into them, and say them with the right spirit of intent. Keep that spirit strong as you go through the affirmation process, as deep-rooted change is a step-by-step process that takes time.

Making deep-rooted change takes time and internalizing your affirmations takes time. For most of us, change happens gradually, in increments, so I encourage you to be patient with your efforts and persist in them. As a rule, change requires many iterations and repetitions before it "takes" in your subconscious and your internal picture changes.

Says Who?

Once the change is recorded firmly and solidly in your subconscious and constantly reinforced, it is not easily erased. So, don't be discouraged if you don't see results immediately. Keep repeating your affirmations daily, and remember to read, picture, and feel them, as vividly as possible. The process will better assist you in remaining focused on your goals, even in the midst of a storm.

Chapter 26
Expand Your Comfort Zone

Making and keeping commitments plays a vital role in our ability to remain focused on our goals.

The word *commitment* is commonly used. We often hear people ask, "Will you commit to me." A young couple may be dating and one or the other may comment, "I am looking for a *commitment* from you."

The mere mention of the word may make the other person feel uncomfortable, especially if they feel they are not ready for the commitment being requested of them.

For some people, putting their goals in writing is a challenge, perhaps because they believe that if they put their goals in writing, they must then commit to them, and they feel they aren't ready to commit at that level yet.

In both examples, the "commitment" poses the greatest degree of discomfort. That's because of the possibility that the commitment will cause them to venture into unknown territory. It will cause them to venture outside of their comfort zone.

Right or Uptight?

So, have you ever asked yourself, "Why do I sometimes feel right at home in certain situations or settings, but at other times I'm uptight, tense, and uncomfortable? What's the problem? Is it the situation, or is it me?" The answer is simple: When you're tense and uptight, you're out of your comfort zone.

Says Who?

A comfort zone is any time or place where you feel comfortable, calm, and relaxed. It's regulated by your self-image. If you see yourself as capable, confident, and able to adapt to any situation, your comfort zone will be very broad. If your dominant self-image is one of self-doubt, inferiority and incompetence, you will have a more rigid, narrow, and confining comfort zone.

Whenever you try to operate outside of your comfort zone without first expanding your self-image, your performance suffers. You become so full of anxiety that all you want to do is get back to where you feel most comfortable. Even if you desire something better, your discomfort is so strong that you abandon your vision and return quickly to your current reality.

At certain times and in certain situations, you may feel uncomfortable or out of place. Perhaps you experience such discomfort when you are asked to speak in front of a group, interview for a job, make a sales call to a new prospect, learn a new software program, or try to meet a deadline at work. Maybe you feel uncomfortable when you attend a party where you don't know anyone.

In more familiar situations, you feel relaxed, calm, and comfortable. You feel you can be yourself, because of your self-regulating comfort zone.

For every belief you hold about yourself in current reality, there is a corresponding comfort zone. While you're in it, you know how to behave and what is expected of you. When you're out of it, you feel anxiety and stress, and this feeling can cause you to lose focus and concentration on your goals. Your hands may become sweaty; your breathing may become rapid and shallow; your muscles may become tense; your voice may crack; and your ability to express yourself in words may fail.

Automatic Pilot

Your self-image operates like an automatic pilot on a boat or airplane. When you program it to operate within certain boundaries, you can walk away and leave the controls. If the boat or plane veers slightly off course, the automatic pilot will bring it back to where it belongs, on course as programmed. It will continue to operate smoothly and automatically within the selected zone until you change the programming.

Your comfort zone operates in a similar manner as the automatic pilot on a boat or airplane, with one exception. Instead of an automatic pilot that determines where and when you operate smoothly, you have a self-image. The higher your self-esteem and the more positive your self-image, the broader your comfort zone will be. If you are confident of your ability to adapt to new situations, you'll feel more comfortable in a variety of places. If you doubt yourself and your capacity to handle something new and different, your comfort zone will be very narrow.

Expand the Zone

One key to improving your capability of remaining focused on your goals while in the storm is to expand your comfort zone.

I have a comfort zone, and you have a comfort zone. Highly effective people and high-performance individuals have a comfort zone, although their comfort zones are broader than most.

How we value ourselves and how we perform are controlled by our self-image, and the comfort zone we create that matches this picture. Moving out of our comfort zone causes tension and anxiety. We feel out of place, both physically and emotionally. We are unable to think and act as we normally do. This discomfort drives us to get back into the range where we feel most comfortable.

Says Who?

You have many comfort zones. For every truth you have, for each current self-image you have, there is a corresponding comfort zone. As long as you live, work, and function close to your image of yourself, you will effectively and efficiently perform tasks and skills in this area. Performing outside of your comfort zone usually lowers your performance and causes anxiety and stress.

When you move away from your currently dominant self-image in a corresponding area of effectiveness, you experience both physical and psychological feedback. You are unable to think and act as you normally do. The feeling of being out of place, physically and emotionally, causes you to get back into that range where you feel more comfortable.

Feelings of stress and anxiety serve as internal subconscious regulators, causing you to get back to where you think you belong. To eliminate stress and anxiety, learn to visualize yourself in a new situation. You can do this safely. Visualize yourself in the next income level safely. Visualize yourself leading your company into a better production schedule. Visualize a higher quality in all areas of your life.

Because of your self-image pictures and comfort zones, you automatically act as you see yourself to be. The action is automatic, a subconscious check-and-balance system. So if you desire to change the way you act, change the way you think, and your performance will follow. The process of expanding your comfort zone will assist you in remaining focused on your goals when you find yourself in the storm.

Section 7
Maintain Faith in the Storm

What sustaining forces can you tap into when you face a storm? In this last section, I suggest that there are four such forces available to you. These four forces enable you to be your best in spite of circumstances: self-esteem, self-confidence, faith, and positive expectations.

Chapter 27
Self-Esteem: The Power to Be Your Best

Being the best you can be involves many steps. Taking steps daily to grow personally and professionally and enhancing your skill-set can aid you in becoming the best you can be. Also, you enhance your self-esteem when you don't buy into critical comments you hear from others that are not in alignment with your vision, mission, and values.

One way to accomplish this is to "put the brakes" on the negative thoughts created in your mind as a result of comments you hear from others. You may do so by asking "Says who?" when inquiring why you may be thinking the way you're thinking.

I also encourage you to ask yourself. "Where do those thoughts come from, and how can I change them, if they are out of alignment with my vision, mission, and values in life?" This process will further assist you in enhancing your self-esteem.

High Self-Esteem

Developing and maintaining high self-esteem is a vital part of being the best you can be. It's the sense of your worthiness, your competence, or your ability to cope with the basic challenges of life in a constructive way. It's your reputation you have with yourself.

Having high self-esteem means that you appreciate your own worth and importance and that you have the character to be accountable for your actions. That includes setting realistic expectations, taking risks, trusting, and knowing that you can remain true to your principles, no matter what life sends your way. It also means placing a high value on your creativity, your mind and body, and your purpose in life.

Having high self-esteem doesn't mean you feel good about yourself every minute of the day. That is unrealistic. If you fall below your standards or hurt someone else, you naturally feel bad about it. If you make a big mistake, it's natural to feel some self-doubt. But when you have a high self-esteem, painful feelings tend to pass quickly. You believe that you can learn and grow from your problems or mistakes and that you are essentially a good person who deserves success and happiness. You believe it, not because you are arrogant, but because you behave in ways that create this belief.

What Do You Believe?

You were not born with the level of self-esteem you have today. You started developing your self-esteem during childhood as you listened to authority figures share with you their opinions and perceptions about you. People with low self-esteem aren't born that way. They usually become that way by hearing critical messages from authority figures telling them over and over, in words and through their actions, that they are not "good enough," "smart enough," or "can't do anything right." When you are a child, anyone older than you is an authority figure.

If you hear that you're bad, stupid, clumsy, hopeless, and worthless enough times, after a while you begin to believe it. You incorporate those opinions into your own self-image and you begin to tell yourself the same demeaning, devaluing messages. And you begin to behave in self-destructive ways, and by the time you're an adult, depression, apathy, substance abuse, violence, or other forms of self-neglect may become part of your life.

High Here, Low There

You can have high self-esteem in some areas and low self-esteem in others. You tend to be very critical of yourself in the areas in which your self-esteem is low. You may even deny that you have any problems at all.

It's difficult to live or work around people with low self-esteem. They are constantly seeking to pull other people down to their level by putting others down and trying to make them look bad. They do it to make themselves look better, so they can feel powerful and in charge, but it doesn't work. Inside their false front of superiority, they feel inferior and worth less than those around them. They can't validate the good in other people because they can't do it for themselves. They have been invalidated so often that they have become emotionally disabled.

High Esteem Is Freedom

When you have high self-esteem, you can express your needs and desires clearly and behave in ways that respect the needs of others without sacrificing your own needs or lowering your standards. High self-esteem enables you to say "no" when others are saying "yes" to things such as drug use or other things that are not in alignment with your vision, mission, and values. It also enables you to take the risks you need to take in order to grow and remain focused on your goals.

High self-esteem gives you the freedom to develop and utilize more of your potential. It gives you the ability to admit your mistakes and weaknesses and develop a proactive approach to life that will bring you success and happiness. If your self-esteem is low, you'll think you don't need to change or can't change, and you may not even try to change. If you don't believe you deserve the best life

has to offer, creating the drive and energy to remain focused on your goals is a more difficult process.

The higher your self-image and self-esteem, the higher the goals you set and achieve. Being your best means being able to better remain focused on your goals, even in storms.

Chapter 28
Self-Confidence:
The Power to Do Your Best

There's something special about being the best you can be as a result of high self-esteem. There's something extraordinary special about being and doing your best when you find yourself in a storm. The more confident you are in pursuing your goals, the more likely you will utilize more of your God-given potential. The more confident you are while pursuing your goals, the more likely you will achieve your vision and mission.

The Webster's dictionary defines *self-confidence* as "belief in oneself and one's powers or abilities." Much of the *Says Who?* approach to life deals with our personal growth and development and the improvement of focus and confidence in our lives. We work on improving ourselves from the inside. We learn to focus our time, efforts, and energies within our *circle of focus*. If something falls in our *area of no control*, we do not focus on it.

However, at one time or another in your life, you may feel that you have the ideal plan and are taking all the right steps, but the results you desire are nowhere to be found. You try to remain focused and confident in your goals; however, the desired results are nowhere to be found. You may then ask yourself, "How much longer can I stay with this plan? Because it's not working for me."

In a slump, you usually suffer a loss of self-confidence. And your loss of self-confidence hinders your ability to perform with excellence on demand. You may even indulge in self-pity and play the role of the victim.

Why Me? Why Not Me?

When challenges, tough circumstances, and stormy weather show up in your life, they can cause you to question your ability to be the best you can be and do the best you can do. They also can leave you asking the question; "Why me?" The mere nature of the storms in your life can test the depth of your faith and confidence. When your faith and confidence are being tested, there are usually three primary areas you tend to question:

1. *You question yourself.* You begin to ask yourself if you have what it takes to achieve the goals you desire in life, or even if you want them if you were to realize them. You lose faith and confidence in yourself.

2. *You question the process.* You begin to have questions about the process or systems you're utilizing to achieve the desired results. You begin to look at all those things on the outside of you, looking for ways to effectively deal with the storms in your life.

3. *You question the presence of God.* You ask yourself, "Why me?" You may feel that you've had your fair share of storms in your life and wonder why are you still encountering life challenges.

God has a plan for each of us. The plan He has for you has not changed. Maybe you've just encountered a storm in your life, and if you are able to turn the circumstances surrounding the storm over to God and refocus on those things you have control over in your life, you begin the process of regaining faith and confidence in yourself and the process you're utilizing to realize your vision. For that reason, I ask "Why not you?" By taking proactive steps to overcome the circumstances you encounter in life, you may encounter special blessings just around the corner.

Calm, Cool, and Confident

What is the ideal state of mind to consistently perform at your best, regardless of the circumstances you find yourself in. For world-class athletes and other highly effective people, a combination of being focused and energized, yet calm, cool, confident, and faithful creates an ideal state of mind to perform at your best.

What separates the world-class performers from others who perform at a lower level is their ability to maintain the ideal state of mind for a longer period of time and their ability to not allow the storms that enter their lives to knock them off their goal.

As you journey through life, you encounter tough circumstances, things not going as planned, and comments from others that are not in alignment with your vision. These circumstances create storms in your life. They add chaos to a life already filled with drama and adventure. How calm, cool, confident, and faithful you remain while in the storm will determine how well you remain focused on your goals.

You see, it's easy to maintain the ideal mindset when the weather conditions reflect sunny skies and 72 degrees outside. However, how calm, cool, confident, and faithful you remain when you're in the storms will affect your state of mind and performance.

You may not really know the depth of your faith or the degree of your self-confidence until you find yourself in the midst of a storm. In fact, you may never know, unless you find yourself in a situation where you are put to the test. How you react at those moments of truth will provide you and those around you with a glimpse of whom you really see yourself to be on the inside and the depth of your faith. This is when you see a sneak preview of your true sub-conscious beliefs.

During storms, your deep-seated beliefs and true character traits rise to the surface. In such times, your ability to remain focused, energized, faithful, calm, cool, and confident is tested. This is when you come to know whether you truly believe in who you say you are as a person or whether you've only been pretending to be someone or something on the outside you're not on the inside.

Adversity is where superstars are made. This is where the likes of Michael Jordan, Tiger Woods, Joe Montana, John Elway, Peyton Manning, Steve Young, and other great sports legends have made their name. They have done so by remaining focused, energized, faithful, calm, cool, and confident in executing their plan of action against tough opposition.

People who remain focused, energized, faithful, calm, cool and confident perform more consistently over time, remain more focused on their goals, and approach life with more drive, energy and motivation. The more focused, calm, cool, and confident you are in pursuing your goals and living your life, the more likely you are to remain focused on your goals, while others may be easily knocked off of their goals.

For example, when I played football for the Los Angeles Rams, we approached a game from a standpoint that there are about 150 total plays combined by both teams, when you add in offense, defense, and special-team plays. When you analyze the outcome of the game, usually only one or two plays determine who wins and who loses the game. That is the case no matter what the final score is. The challenge for the players is that they do not know which of the plays will determine the outcome of the game. Therefore, the elite players approach each and every play of the game with the same mindset, as if that play will be the one to make the difference. This better positions them to make the key plays during a critical period of the game, when the stakes are highest.

Great players tend to make these vital plays at the most critical juncture of the game. They expect to make the play that will make the difference in the game. They have visualized the situation over and over in their minds, so much so that when it's time to actually make the play, they are focused, faithful, energized, calm, cool and confident, which makes for an ideal state of mind to perform at their best.

Since there are about 150 total plays in the game but only one or two make the difference in the game, you may not know in real time which plays will be the ones that make the difference. So, world-class athletes approach each and every play as if it's the play that will determine the final outcome of the game. They approach every play of the game in a focused, energized, calm, cool, confident, and faithful manner.

With this approach, they seek to remain in an ideal state of mind, focused only on those things they can control, like making the play. They leave the results of the play and the outcome up to God, while maintaining faith and remaining calm, cool, and confident—ready for anything that may come their way.

Top sales professionals approach their profession in a similar manner and state of mind. Once they align their daily activities with their marketing plan, they conduct those activities in a focused, faithful, energized, calm, cool, and confident manner. If their game plan calls for them to make 100 sales contacts for the month, they approach each and every one of the contacts as if it is the one that will make a positive difference in them achieving their goals.

Says Who?

With this approach, they remain in an ideal state of mind, focused only on those things they can control—like making the sales call. The results of the call and the outcome, they leave up to God, maintaining faith and remaining calm, cool, and confident—ready for anything that may come their way. This approach will better enable you to remain focused on your goals in the midst of a storm.

Chapter 29
Faith in God:
The Power to Pass the Test

When storms blow into your life from all directions, your faith is tested, and you may be tempted to give up on your goals.

You may try to overcome these challenges and tests and loss of self-confidence by looking for all the answers inside of you.

It is at this point where we can learn a great deal from observing highly effective people. As focused and confident as they may be, when they encounter some of these forces in their lives, they tend to turn to their faith in God to help them through. They do all they can do within their power to overcome the obstacles or barriers standing between them and their vision; however, if they feel that the problem is bigger than they are, they turn it over to God. They then focus their time, effort, and energies on areas over which they have control. They allow God to do His best work.

The decision to turn things over which they have no control over to God puts them in a better position to be the best that they can be. Their faith also enables them to remain focused on the things they have control of and to remain focused on their goals.

If you're looking for a reason to justify your failure to achieve your goals, you will find it—there is an excuse around every corner. You encounter difficult situations each day that can lead to a storm.

You will accomplish a whole lot more good in this world if you consistently use the wonderful gifts and talents you have been granted from God and properly align your vision, mission, and values with your beliefs, habits, attitudes, and expectations in life.

This alignment will take you a long way in life—up to the point where God may step into your life and test the depth of your faith.

Let's look at the *Bible* definition of faith in Hebrews 11:1: "Faith is the substance of things hoped for, the evidence of things not seen."

So having faith means believing in something without seeing it. My Mom taught me another *Bible* truth from Hebrews 11:6: "Without faith, it is impossible to please God, for he who comes to God must believe that He is, and that He rewards those who diligently seek Him."

Based on my beliefs, faith is all about pleasing God. We might have confidence in a person, a game plan or system, but faith is about our belief in God and our desire to please Him. We show our faith when we place our trust in God, especially during storms when we need Him the most.

For many of us, the road from current reality to vision is long and filled with many obstacles or barriers that can knock us off our goal. Some of these obstacles show up in the form of things not going as planned, based on our expectations, causing us to question everything from ourselves to the methods and plans we use to achieve our goals. On certain occasions, the storms we encounter in life will be so powerful they stop us squarely in our tracks. Such moments of truth will test our faith.

A Hand From God in the Storm

I first met Kirk Collins when I played football for the University of Texas. Kirk played football for Baylor University. We were both drafted the same year by the Rams and both played defensive back.

As a number one draft pick, I was fortunate to earn a starting position my rookie year in the league. Kirk had to wait four years to become a starter.

In his first year as a starter, Kirk played exceptionally well in the beginning of the season. After just four games, he was leading the NFL in interceptions. Then he was diagnosed with terminal cancer and was given just six months to live.

At this time, I had lots of questions. First, I asked, "Why Kirk?" I wondered why such a great person with tremendous physical gifts and talents was suddenly hit by such devastating news: just six months to live.

I also questioned the timing. "Of all times, why now? Why did this have to happen when things are going so well for him and his family?"

Being a very private person, Kirk wanted to keep his illness a private matter, even though this was difficult, being in the public eye. He desired to spend most of his remaining time with his wife and family and with me and Leroy Irvin, since the three of us came into the league together and had become the best of friends.

Needless to say, this was a difficult time for Kirk's family, his teammates, and the entire Rams organization. Although Kirk, Leroy and I were strong believers in God, we continued to wonder, "Why Kirk?" and "Why now?"

As time passed, we prayed as friends and as a team for Kirk. We continued to remain faithful and completely turned Kirk's illness over to The Good Lord.

Kirk passed away just five months after learning of his illness at age 26. In my last words to him, I promised him that I would do everything in my power to make sure his name lives on forever. I told him that if I had a son, I would name him Kirk in memory of him.

Kirk was an only son, and his father was in his seventies at the

time of his death. Six months prior to being diagnosed with cancer, Kirk and his wife Ruby were blessed with a son. Later, my wife and I would have our first-born son, whom we named Kirk. Eighteen months later, we were blessed with another boy, whom we named Collin. With that my commitment to my friend Kirk Collins before his death was complete, as our boys bear the names Kirk and Collin in memory of my good friend Kirk Collins. Later, Julie and I were blessed with the girl we desired in Camille.

Although, we had many questions at that time about the timing of many things that took place surrounding Kirk and his illness, had it not been for the faith of The Good Lord, the Collin's bloodline would have ended with Kirk.

I believe that The Good Lord blessed the Johnson household with two wonderful boys and a girl, in part, to enable me to honor my commitment to name my boys after my good friend.

So, if the storm is more than you can handle, I encourage you to focus only on those things you have control of and turn those things you can't control over to God. In the midst of the storm, there's only so much you can do. I encourage you to remain patient and faithful, as the storm will ultimately pass. Your faith will enable you to remain focused on your goals.

Chapter 30
Positive Expectations
The Power to Believe the Best

Have you ever noticed that people who expect the best tend to get it? They expect life to go well for them, and it usually does.

When they have to cope with obstacles, barriers or setbacks along the way, they persist in their efforts, because they expect to succeed in the end. They seem to learn from setbacks or past experiences, and they are stronger and more resilient as a result. When they succeed, they give themselves a pat on the back, because they know they deserve it. And they affirm themselves by saying things like "That's like me!"

Highly effective people or individuals who utilize more of their natural-born potential have a success habit of using positive self-talk to build and strengthen an already positive self-image. They expect the best!

On the other hand, people who are constantly expecting trouble and failure seem to get what they expect, to. When things are going well for them, they worry about when trouble will strike again. When they fail, they're not surprised, because they've been expecting it all along. If they happen to succeed, they attribute it to luck, and they quickly return to their usual poor performance, and they say to themselves "That's just like me."

Expect the Best

While you can't control many of the circumstances in your life, you can learn to control your reaction to them and control of your self-talk. You can learn to think and talk to yourself in ways that will make you much more effective. You can learn to expect the best. When you do, you will be able to utilize more of your potential and remain focused on your goal while in the storm.

Every time you think or speak well of yourself, every time you sincerely praise, encourage or appreciate something about yourself, you are building your self-esteem. You are building a strong, confident self-image. Positive self-talk reinforces your positive self-image, and makes it much more likely that you will utilize more of your potential and perform well again.

Build Confidence

Negative self-talk has an opposite effect. Every time you belittle, devalue or put yourself down, you are chipping away at your self-image. Negative self-talk undermines your self-image and makes it more likely that you'll perform poorly again.

Expecting the best affirms that you have confidence in yourself and faith in God to handle those things which are out of your control. Expecting the best enhances your believe in yourself and your abilities to meet challenges and deal constructively with obstacles and setbacks.

When something happens that you don't expect, you are confident enough to handle it. If you find yourself in the midst of challenges, even very serious ones, you know you can weather the storm. You pick yourself up, dust yourself off, and start all over again, knowing that you gained knowledge and wisdom from the experience and that you have what it takes to succeed. When a challenge seems bigger than you are, you don't quit on your goal, you turn it over to God and resolve to grow bigger than it is.

When you expect the best, you affirm your ability to remain focused on your goals, despite your circumstances, things not going as planned for you, or negative comments you hear from others. Expecting the best means becoming solution-focused, instead of problem-focused. You don't spend much time thinking about what's wrong. Instead, you acknowledge the problems, analyze them, and focus your mental energy on what you want it to look like when the problem no longer exists.

Forge Your Future

Your present thoughts determine your future. If you spend all of your time focused on what's wrong, worrying about the bad things that might happen, dreading the future, those are the images you are sending to your subconscious. You are making negative affirmations; you are visualizing trouble and terrible results. So what do you think you are likely to see more of in the future? You will see trouble and terrible results.

Many things in this world are beyond your control; I encourage you to turn those things over to God. But there is one very important thing that you have total control over, and that is what goes into your mind. You can take charge of your thoughts and self-talk. You can make sure that your self-talk consists of hopeful, confident, self-affirming expectation of a future you can get excited about.

When you exercise control over your self-talk, you build a positive self-image that will create opportunities, open doors, and move mountains, enabling you to remain energized, calm, cool, confident, faithful and focused while in the storm.

Postscript
The Adventures of Life

As you apply these principles consistently in your life, you will see some very positive changes. You will feel more powerful than you have ever felt before and remain focused on your goals and utilize more of your natural potential to benefit yourself and others.

As a focused, fearless and faithful person, you will feel more confident about bringing your vision for the future into reality. With God's guidance, you will have a growing sense of being in control of your own life. It won't happen like magic overnight, but it will happen.

You now have the knowledge that, if consistently applied, will enable you to remain focused on your goals. When you take full accountability for your own life, and consistently follow the steps, there are no limits to what you can accomplish in life. You also have what it takes to inspire and encourage others in ways that allow them to rise above self-doubt and pursue their greatest ambitions, without focusing on the limitations set by others.

This doesn't mean your life will become a fairy tale fantasy. You will still experience some challenges, obstacles, barriers, or setbacks along the way. There will likely be times when you'll wonder if your goals are too high. At other times you may be tempted to throw in the towel and quit. No doubt, there will be times when your commitments to your goals will waiver. But, these are the times when this information will become even more valuable. If

you maintain the faith in the storm, you gain additional knowledge and wisdom to better enable you to realize more of your vision and mission in life.

You can't control everything that happens in your life, but you can control your response to what happens. Every setback you face can be turned into a springboard with the knowledge and wisdom you gain with each setback. Tough times can make you stronger. You can weather any storm and be a better person as a result if you control your self-talk; keep your purpose, mission, and vision in focus; and take accountability for your actions during the tough times.

The tools you now have available to you and the knowledge you now possess are powerful. But if you don't use them, it won't matter. If you use the affirmation and visualization process correctly, setbacks may still occur; however, you'll see them as temporary and find your way around, over, past, or through them. Sure, you'll come up against a locked door every now and then, but you'll have the key.

The more of your God-given potential you use, the more you can help other people grow and deal more effectively with the challenges they may face. When you share what you learn with others, when you firmly believe in their ability to grow and remind them of their great strengths and potential, you'll be a powerful force in the development of their potential. You'll help them to believe in themselves and utilize more of their God-given potential. And you'll help the world be a more productive and better place to live for all of us.

Proceeds Benefit Hurricane Victims

"World Class Coaches" has made a $500,000 pledge to the United Way Hurricane Relief and Recovery Fund from the proceeds of "Says Who?". To learn more about the fund and how you can help rebuild communities affected by the 2005 hurricane season, or improve your community through your local United Way, go to www.unitedway.org.

World Class Coaches

"Our mission is to empower individuals to achieve their God-given potential and significantly increase their performance capability by recognizing their ability to choose personal and professional growth in order to achieve personal and professional excellence."

The Growing Tree World Class Coaching Programs
Helping you climb the steps to achieve personal growth and success.

Growing Tree Learning Center, produces worldclasscoaches.com. The company is an International Educational Company, offering individuals and organizations educational tools and services to maximize their potential. The company is dedicated to providing the highest quality of service in the personal growth and development industry and helping our clients achieve their God-given potential and realize their goals.

The company provides world-class coaching programs, seminars, workshops and consulting services that enhance personal and organizational performance in the areas of SALES, LEADERSHIP, TEAMWORK, COMMUNICATION, MOTIVATION, AND LIFE MANAGEMENT SKILLS. To inquire about personal coaches or to schedule a speaker contact us at:

Growing Tree Learning Center, Inc.
DBA World Class Coaches
3540 W. Sahara Ave. #780
Las Vegas, NV 89102
www.worldclasscoaches.com
800-314-7713
Fax 702-920-7655

Growing Tree Learning Center, Inc.
affiliate of Performance Research International, Inc.

WORLD CLASS COACHES

What might be holding you back from achieving more of your full potential?

What might be keeping you from getting what you want in life?

What is one thing you have not done because you were intimidated or afraid?

Did you ever attend a heart-pounding, soul-stirring motivational seminar and leave feeling highly motivated ... only to have that wonderful euphoric feeling disappear after a few days? Do you have a piece of exercise equipment or an audio tape series that you bought and never used?

Sounds like you can benefit from the same thing that world-class athletes and other highly successful individuals benefit from a personal coach!

Everyone dreams of what can be. The Growing Tree World Class Coaching System™ shows you how to turn those dreams into reality.

Growing Tree Learning Center, Inc.
affiliate of Performance Research International, Inc.

Benefit from the same proven techniques and strategies that have helped many others improve their productivity. Our Coaching Programs are designed to help you reach the next level in your life and business career.

With the Growing Tree Personal Coaching System, you receive:

▷ Personalized coaching by your coach.

▷ Assessment of the current status of your personal and professional life.

▷ Assistance in mapping out your personal and professional goals by building your "Personal Empowerment Process Model."

▷ Assistance in helping you to develop a precise business plan to achieve your goals.

▷ Assistance in developing the necessary soft and hard skills to realize goals.

▷ Assistance in identifying and practicing the fundamentals necessary to achieve your goals.

▷ Personal guidance, instruction and encouragement to keep you on track to achieving your goals through intensive accountability.

▷ Cutting-edge strategies for success in today's marketplace.

▷ The keys to scheduling and successful time management.

▷ How to develop the success habits and attitude of the business.

▷ Keys to on-going business generation.

For more details on our services/programs, contact a World Class Coaches representative by calling 1-800-314-9750 or sending an e-mail to info@worldclasscoaches.com

www.worldclasscoaches.com

Why invest $8 to $10 a month in your own leadership development?

You will receive an exponential return on investment.

For the past 20 years, our three monthly magazines have been the best source for the best and brightest insights from all the top consultants, coaches, authors, and speakers on team leadership and personal development.

Now you can subscribe to *Executive Excellence, Sales and Service Excellence* or *Personal Excellence* at a special discounted rate of 25 percent!

Team Leadership ($10/month)
Executive Excellence brings together the best thinking in the world on all the issues that leaders encounter, and of fers it all in the most time-effective format.

Sales/Service Leadership ($8/month)
Sales and Service Excellence covers seven dimensions of sales, marketing, and service excellence.

Self-leadership ($8/month)
Personal Excellence focuses on seven dimensions of personal and professional leadership.

There's more! To help you get the most out of your favorite articles and implement new ideas you will also receive FREE:

The *Personal Excellence Plan,* an easy-to-use guide designed to help you create and implement a vision and mission, goals and priorities.

Excellence in Action, found at the end of each article to motivate to implement the insights the author has shared. In addition, we provide you with an *Excellence in Action Guide* to help you put into action those ideas that will bring about desired change.

Executive Excellence Worksheet, the perfect way to bring *Executive Excellence* or *Personal Excellence* into a meeting or team. It's designed to bring focus and vision to your team.

Certificate of Excellence, the best way to recognize and reward people. Use the Executive Excellence Performance System now to bring about desired change!

Executive Excellence
(print or audio)
One-year subscription $119
*(4 to 9 subscription are $80 each
10 to 24 are $60 each
25 to 99 are $50 each
100+ are $40 each)*
Electronic Subscription: $10 each
*Group discounts as low as
$2 per person per year.*

***Sales & Service Excellence
or Personal Excellence***
(print magazine)
One-year subscription $96
*(4 to 9 subscription are $55 each
10 to 24 are $45 each
25 to 99 are $40 each
100+ are $35 each)*
Electronic Subscription: $8 each
*Group discounts as low as
$1 per person per year.*

◀ ***Instant Consultant***
*CD Archive for just $149
It's a coaching and leadership development program on CD ROM.*

*Find a wiser,
better way to
live your life
and lead your
organization.*

Invest wisely. Invest in excellence.
TO ORDER, CALL 801-375-4060.